*This book is dedicated to my wife Elsie, whose patience, understanding, and help mean more to me than words can express*

# MEASURED DRAWINGS
## OF
# SHAKER FURNITURE
### AND
# WOODENWARE

EJNER HANDBERG

The Berkshire Traveller Press
STOCKBRIDGE, MASSACHUSETTS

OTHER BOOKS OF SHAKER INTEREST
FROM THE BERKSHIRE TRAVELLER PRESS:

*Shop Drawings of Shaker Furniture and Woodenware, Volumes
I, II, and III* by Ejner Handberg

*Shop Drawings of Shaker Iron and Tinware* by Ejner Handberg

*Fruits of the Shaker Tree of Life: Memoirs of Fifty Years of
Collecting and Research* by Faith and Edward Deming Andrews

ISBN 0-912944-63-3
Library of Congress 80-67765
Printed in the United States of America by The Studley Press, Inc.,
Dalton, Massachusetts 01226

6 5 4 3

## A TRIBUTE TO THE HANDBERGS

*A native of Denmark, Ejner came to this country as a young man. He applied his skills and rich traditions to the building of houses and study of fine furniture.*

*He and his wife Elsie, a New Englander, have spent most of their life in the Berkshires.*

*Some twenty-five years ago they became interested in the craftsmanship of the Shakers. Their appreciation and study of the sect's furniture led Ejner to the recording of important pieces in private and museum collections, resulting in the publication of four books.*

*This 1980 book by two of the "world's people" is a composite of new findings and choice pieces from earlier studies—offering a timely contribution to the art of the Shakers.*

*Faith Andrews*

*June 7, 1980*

## ACKNOWLEDGMENTS

I wish to express my sincere thanks and appreciation to the following museums and galleries which have given me their permission to make measured drawings of Shaker furniture in their collections:

The Boston Museum of Fine Arts, Boston, Massachusetts
The Hancock Shaker Village, Hancock, Massachusetts
The Shaker Museum, Old Chatham, New York
Shakertown at Pleasant Hill, Harrodsburg, Kentucky
Shakertown at South Union, Kentucky
Canterbury Shaker Museum, East Canterbury, New Hampshire
Green Willow Farm Gallery, Chatham, New York
Charles L. Flint, Antiques, Lenox, Massachusetts

I gratefully acknowledge the valuable information and help given me by Mrs. Edward Deming Andrews, and thank her for permission to make measured drawings of the Andrews collection of Shaker furniture. Above all I am grateful to my wife Elsie for long hours of reading and correcting the text.

# CONTENTS

# INTRODUCTION

At the present time there is a great interest in Shaker furniture and woodenware. Not only does much Shaker furniture have an artistic value, but as the forerunner of our present-day functional furniture it has become a prized possession today. It would not be wrong to claim that some of the so-called Danish-modern furniture designers have used many of the details of Shaker furniture in their original designs.

One cannot make a Shaker reproduction without understanding just a little better the aims of the Shaker cabinetmakers who made them and developing an appreciation of the people who used them. There is a great deal more value to be found from reproducing these pieces than just the handwork involved. Exact reproductions are desirable when the piece copied combines in itself utility and beauty. There is a Shaker saying, "That which has the highest use possesses the greatest beauty."

Shaker furniture was meant to serve the needs of a plain-living people and depended upon simplicity, usefulness, and the best of workmanship for its beauty. There were no fancy turnings or moldings, for the Shakers had only utility in mind. All decorations were forbidden by Shaker laws, yet within these rules the Brethren made useful and beautiful pieces, perfect in workmanship. The lines of the furniture were plain and true, free from all needless elaborations and adornments, with smooth surfaces so they could easily be kept clean. The eventual result was an original, distinct, and different style of furniture, truly functional, combining beauty with utility. "Whatever is made, let it be plain and simple; any ornamentation adds nothing to its goodness or durability." Care was taken that no product which was imperfect in any way be sold to the outside world. They achieved a standard of workmanship that has seldom been equalled since.

# SELECTION AND DRYING OF WOOD

The lumber used for Shaker furniture came mainly from their own land. Almost every Shaker community owned large tracts of woodland rich in timber. Eastern white pine (soft pine) was the most commonly used furniture wood for cases of drawers, cupboards, blanket chests, wood-boxes, benches, washstands, and many other items. Often candlestands, workstands, and sewing stands were made of cherry, maple, or birch with a pine top. One feature in Shaker furniture and woodenware was the use of quarter-sawn edge-grained pine, which is less apt to cup or warp than flat-grained boards. Black cherry, yellow birch, and maple were used in all pieces requiring strength and having to withstand wear, such as table legs, chair posts, and the pedestals and legs of small stands like candlestands, sewing stands, and workstands. Occasionally, small tables, chairs, and the like made entirely of native walnut, maple, or butternut and other native hard and close-grained woods can be seen; also, but less often, one may see them made of bird's-eye maple, curly maple or tiger maple. The Shaker cabinetmakers did not hesitate to use more than one kind of wood in their furniture and woodenware. For example, the table legs might be of cherry, the frame or skirt of maple or birch, and the top of pine. Ash and hickory were used for rockers, rungs, sometimes the slats of chairs, and also parts which were to be steamed and bent.

I cannot stress enough the importance of selecting the very best of lumber for your project and being sure it is properly dried. The use to which the lumber is put determines how much moisture is to be removed in drying. Lumber and furniture exposed to outdoor air need not be dried to as low a moisture content as lumber used for fine furniture which is exposed to the heated indoor air, the moisture content of which must be less than 10%.

If lumber is newly cut, that means it must first be air-dried outside during the summer for six months or more. Air-drying of lumber consists of carefully piling the boards outdoors with stickers laid crosswise between each layer and about three to four feet apart to keep the layers separated. There should be about an inch space between the edges of the boards for air to move up and down through the pile, and the top of the pile must be covered against the rain and sun.

After air-drying, the lumber must be brought inside. A good place is in the loft over the shop or a similar heated place. The time necessary to finish drying depends upon the thickness: about six months or more for one-inch lumber; twice that for two-inch; and so on.

Never dry the surface of a board any faster than the moisture can be drawn out from the center of the board, to prevent splitting and "case-hardening" of the surface.

Even if your lumber has been kiln-dried, but left to build up moisture during humid weather, it must be brought back down to a moisture content of 6% to 8%.

When lumber, particularly soft wood, is dry enough to use, the sawdust will feel very dry to your hands and the shavings from a planer are very brittle. Very dry lumber with less than 5% moisture will swell during humid months if not finished immediately after it is assembled. Now apply several coats of your choice of finish and always the same on the bottom as the top.

For a more accurate guideline to the moisture content of the wood you are thinking of using for fine furniture, cut a sample of no less than ten square inches. Then weigh it very accurately to find its original weight. Then dry the sample in an oven set about 215° until it stops losing weight, and that will be its oven-dry weight. Now subtract the oven-dry weight from the original weight, multiply that by 100, and divide by original weight. The result is the moisture content of original sample.

Example: original weight 10 oz.
oven-dry weight $\underline{\ 8\ }$ oz.

$$2 \text{ oz.} \times 100 = \frac{200}{10} = 20\%$$

# SHAKER-MADE FURNITURE

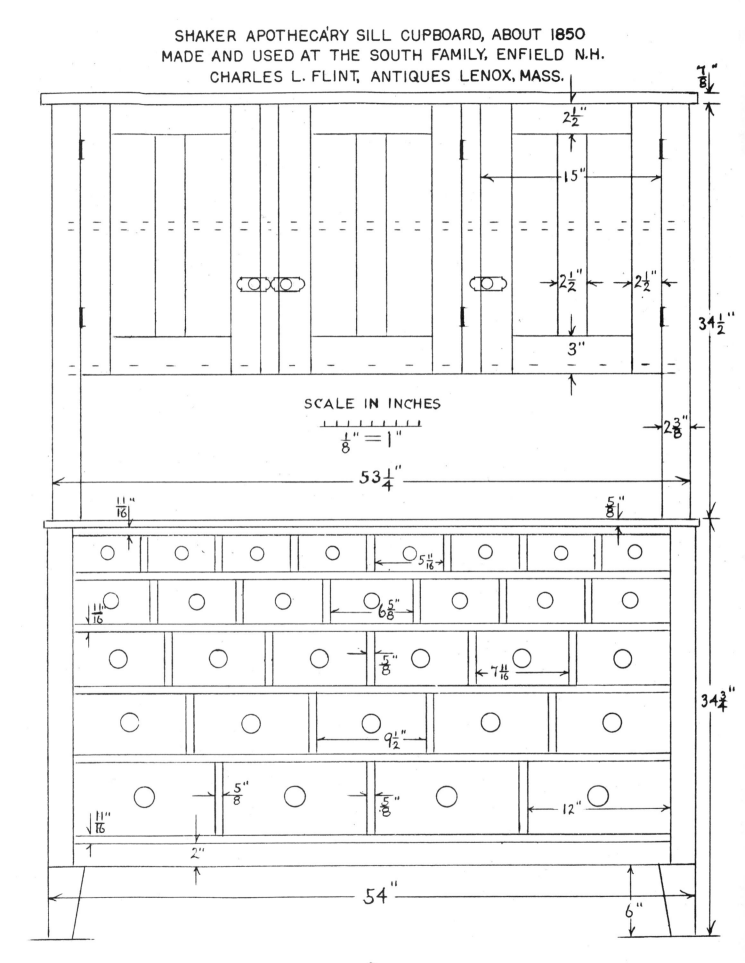

SHAKER APOTHECARY SILL CUPBOARD, ABOUT 1850
MADE AND USED AT THE SOUTH FAMILY, ENFIELD N.H.
CHARLES L. FLINT, ANTIQUES LENOX, MASS.

SCALE IN INCHES

$\frac{1}{8}" = 1"$

2

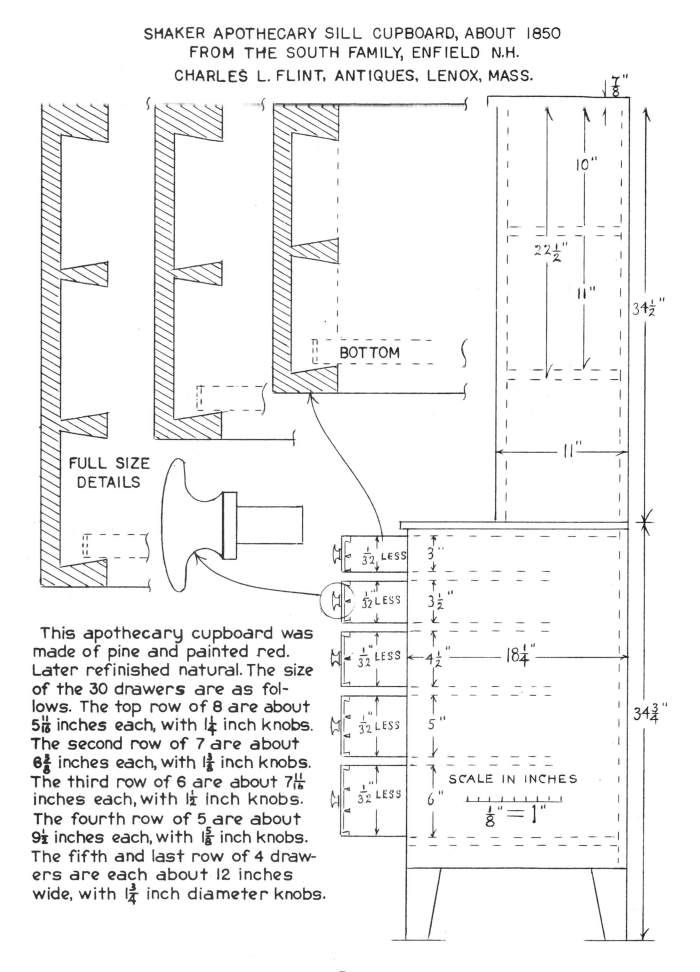

FULL SIZE
DETAILS

BOTTOM

$\frac{7}{8}$"

10"

$22\frac{1}{2}$"

11"

34$\frac{1}{2}$"

11"

$\frac{1}{32}$" LESS    3"

$\frac{1}{32}$" LESS    3$\frac{1}{2}$"

$\frac{1}{32}$" LESS    4$\frac{1}{2}$"    18$\frac{1}{4}$"

$\frac{1}{32}$" LESS    5"    34$\frac{3}{4}$"

$\frac{1}{32}$" LESS    6"

SCALE IN INCHES
$\frac{1}{8}$" = 1"

This apothecary cupboard was
made of pine and painted red.
Later refinished natural. The size
of the 30 drawers are as fol-
lows. The top row of 8 are about
5$\frac{11}{16}$ inches each, with 1$\frac{1}{4}$ inch knobs.
The second row of 7 are about
6$\frac{5}{8}$ inches each, with 1$\frac{3}{8}$ inch knobs.
The third row of 6 are about 7$\frac{11}{16}$
inches each, with 1$\frac{1}{2}$ inch knobs.
The fourth row of 5 are about
9$\frac{1}{2}$ inches each, with 1$\frac{5}{8}$ inch knobs.
The fifth and last row of 4 draw-
ers are each about 12 inches
wide, with 1$\frac{3}{4}$ inch diameter knobs.

# HIGH CUPBOARD CHEST
## THE SHAKER MUSEUM, OLD CHATHAM, N.Y.

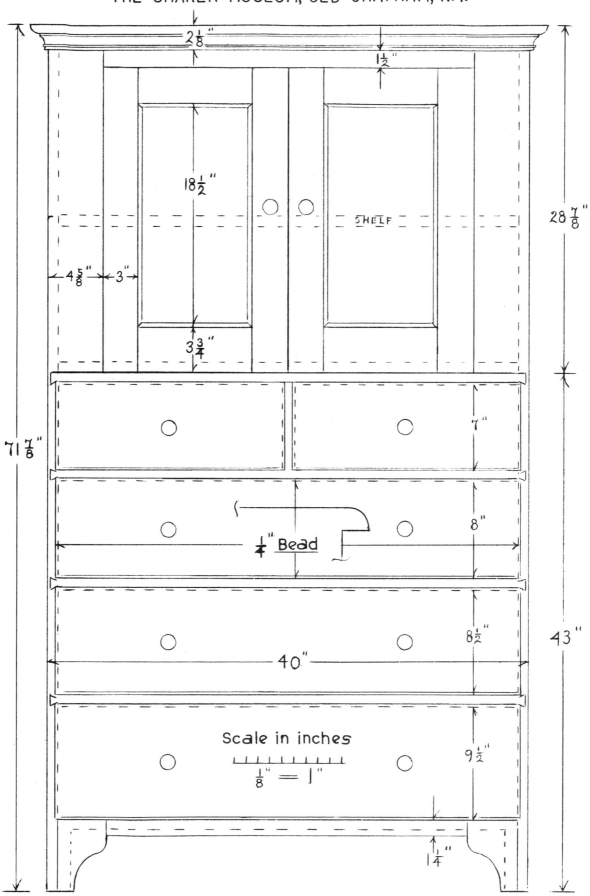

$2\frac{1}{8}$"

$1\frac{1}{2}$"

$18\frac{1}{2}$"

SHELF

$28\frac{7}{8}$"

$4\frac{5}{8}$"  3"

$3\frac{3}{4}$"

7"

8"

$\frac{1}{4}$" Bead

$71\frac{7}{8}$"

$8\frac{1}{2}$"

43"

40"

Scale in inches

$\frac{1}{8}$" = 1"

$9\frac{1}{2}$"

$1\frac{1}{4}$"

4

# HIGH CUPBOARD CHEST
## THE SHAKER MUSEUM, OLD CHATHAM, N.Y.

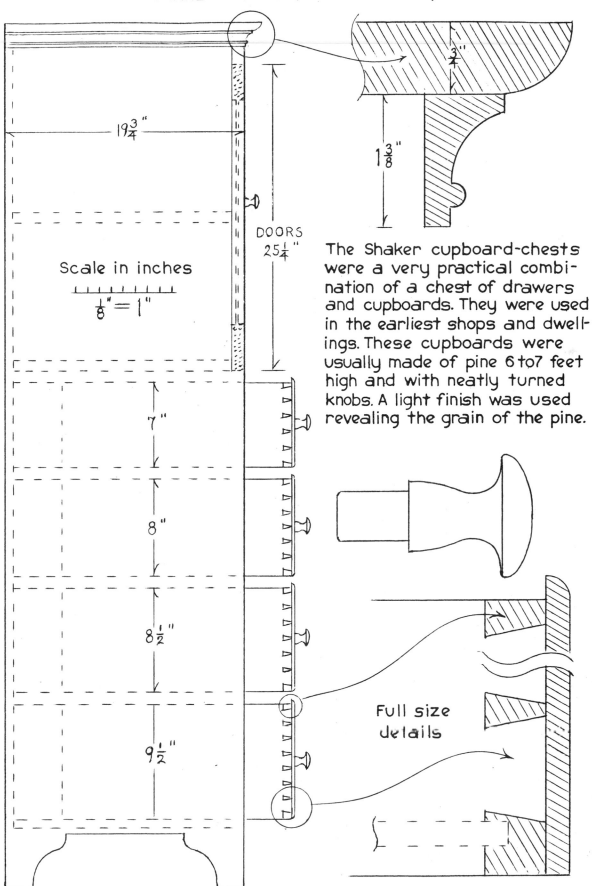

19¾"

Scale in inches

⅛" = 1"

DOORS
25¼"

1⅜"

¾"

7"

8"

8½"

9½"

The Shaker cupboard-chests were a very practical combination of a chest of drawers and cupboards. They were used in the earliest shops and dwellings. These cupboards were usually made of pine 6 to 7 feet high and with neatly turned knobs. A light finish was used revealing the grain of the pine.

Full size details

# CHEST OF DRAWERS, WATERVLIET, N.Y. MARKED 1823
## CHARLES L. FLINT, ANTIQUES, LENOX, MASS.

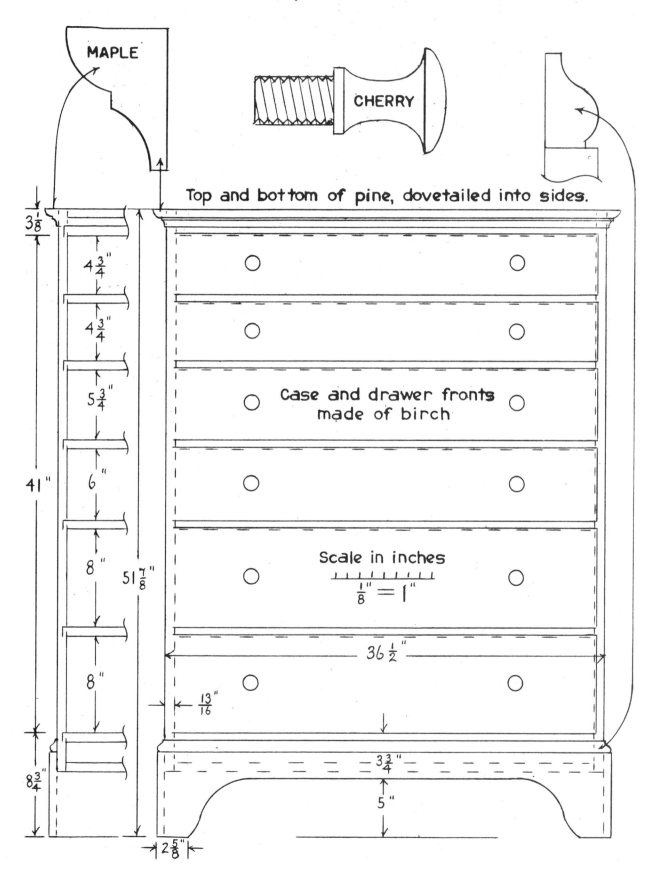

MAPLE

CHERRY

Top and bottom of pine, dovetailed into sides.

$3\frac{1}{8}$

$4\frac{3}{4}$"

$4\frac{3}{4}$"

$5\frac{3}{4}$"

6 "

8 "

8 "

$8\frac{3}{4}$"

41 "

$51\frac{7}{8}$ "

Case and drawer fronts
made of birch

Scale in inches

$\frac{1}{8}$" = 1"

$36\frac{1}{2}$ "

$\frac{13}{16}$"

$3\frac{3}{4}$"

5 "

$2\frac{5}{8}$"

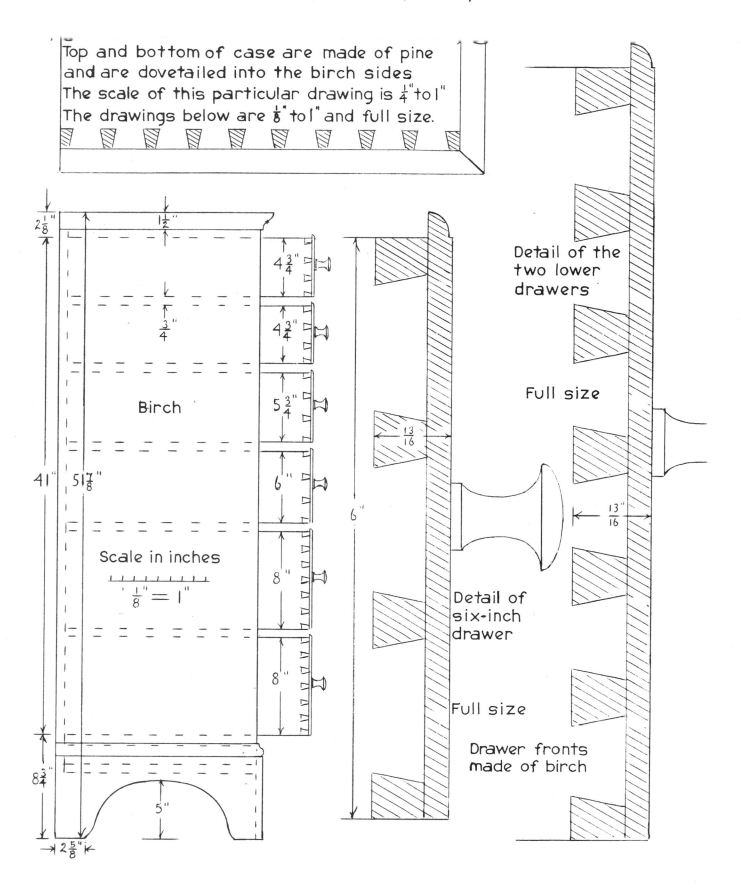

Top and bottom of case are made of pine
and are dovetailed into the birch sides
The scale of this particular drawing is $\frac{1}{4}$" to 1"
The drawings below are $\frac{1}{8}$" to 1" and full size.

$2\frac{1}{8}$"

$1\frac{1}{2}$"

$4\frac{3}{4}$"

$\frac{3}{4}$"

$4\frac{3}{4}$"

Birch

$5\frac{3}{4}$"

$6$"

41"   $51\frac{7}{8}$"

Scale in inches

$8$"

$\frac{1}{8}$" = 1"

$8$"

$8\frac{3}{4}$"

5"

$2\frac{5}{8}$"

Detail of the
two lower
drawers

Full size

$\frac{13}{16}$

$6$"

$\frac{13}{16}$

Detail of
six-inch
drawer

Full size

Drawer fronts
made of birch

# LOW WORK COUNTER, FROM CANTERBURY, N.H. ABOUT 1820
## CHARLES L. FLINT, ANTIQUES, LENOX, MASS.

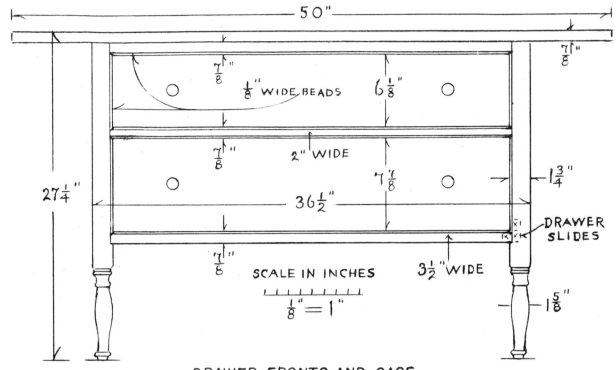

DRAWER FRONTS AND CASE
MADE OF CHERRY, PAINTED,
WITH A TWO-BOARD PINE TOP

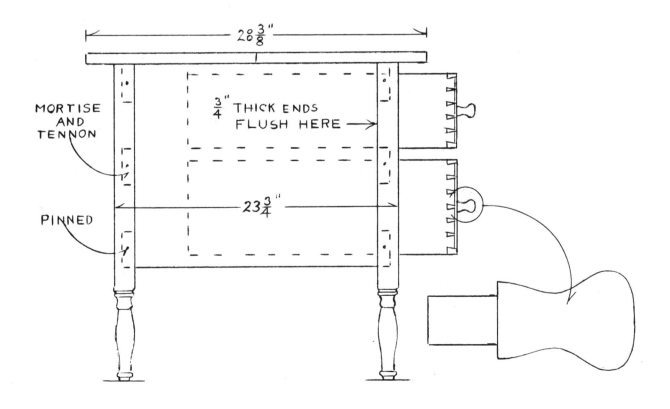

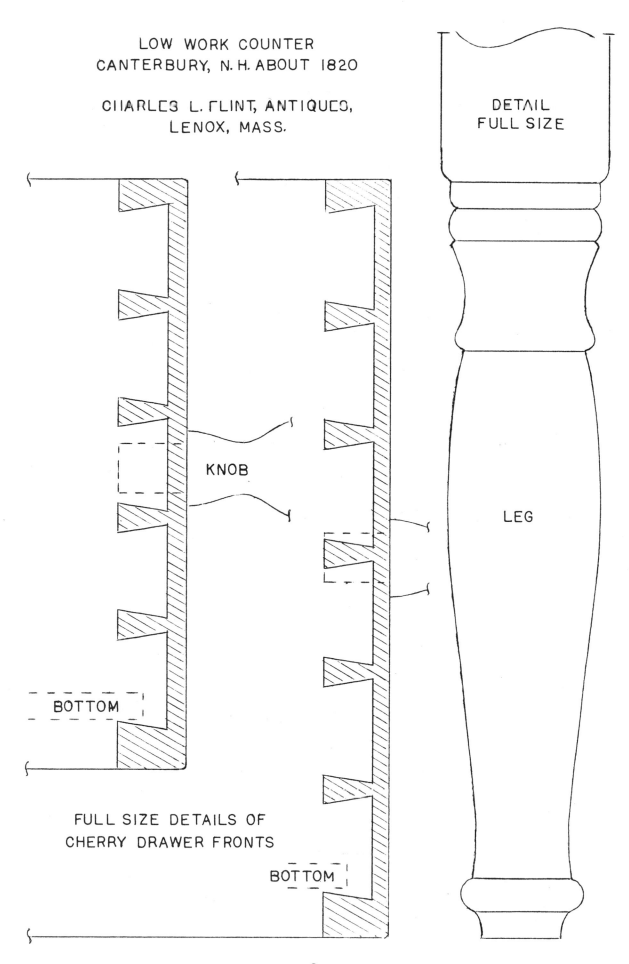

LOW WORK COUNTER
CANTERBURY, N.H. ABOUT 1820

CHARLES L. FLINT, ANTIQUES,
LENOX, MASS.

DETAIL
FULL SIZE

KNOB

LEG

BOTTOM

FULL SIZE DETAILS OF
CHERRY DRAWER FRONTS

BOTTOM

# TAILORESSES' SHOP COUNTER

### FROM ANDREWS COLLECTION

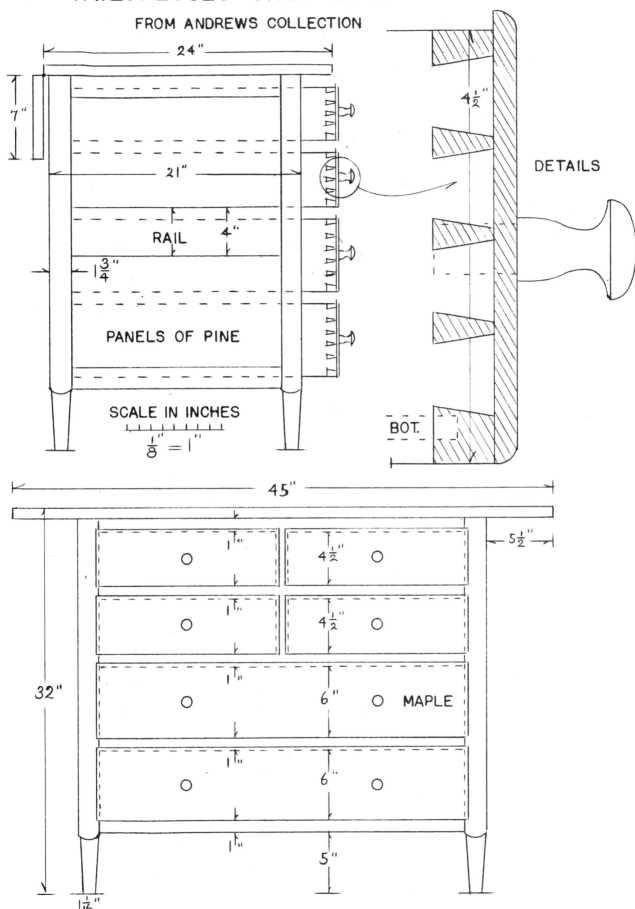

24"

7"

21"

RAIL 4"

$1\frac{3}{4}$"

PANELS OF PINE

SCALE IN INCHES

$\frac{1}{8}$" = 1"

$4\frac{1}{2}$"

DETAILS

BOT.

45"

$5\frac{1}{2}$"

1"

$4\frac{1}{2}$"

1"

$4\frac{1}{2}$"

32"

1"

6"    MAPLE

1"

6"

1"

5"

$1\frac{1}{16}$"

# TAILORESSES' SHOP COUNTER

## FROM ANDREWS COLLECTION

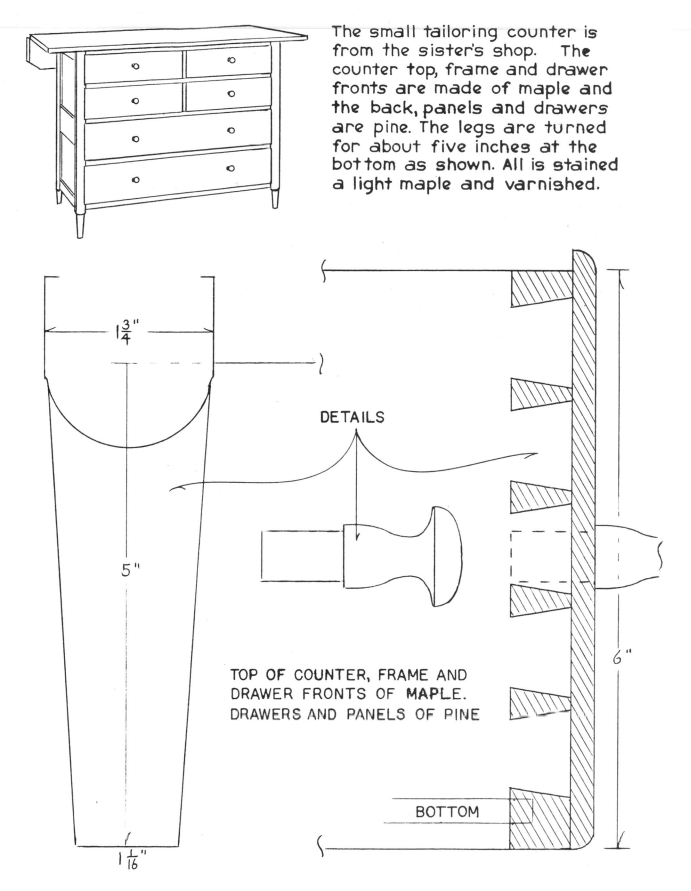

The small tailoring counter is from the sister's shop. The counter top, frame and drawer fronts are made of maple and the back, panels and drawers are pine. The legs are turned for about five inches at the bottom as shown. All is stained a light maple and varnished.

$1\frac{3}{4}$"

5"

$1\frac{1}{16}$"

DETAILS

TOP OF COUNTER, FRAME AND
DRAWER FRONTS OF MAPLE.
DRAWERS AND PANELS OF PINE

BOTTOM

6"

# SEWING DESK

Many different styles of sewing desks, tables or stands were made for the Shaker seamstresses. In the East they were usually made of pine, maple or birch and were very plain. The sewing desks and tables almost always had graduated drawers on the top, bottom and sometimes on the sides. If it had a pull-out slide for sewing or writing, it was called a sewing desk. The pull-out slide should be fitted with breadboard ends to keep it perfectly flat.

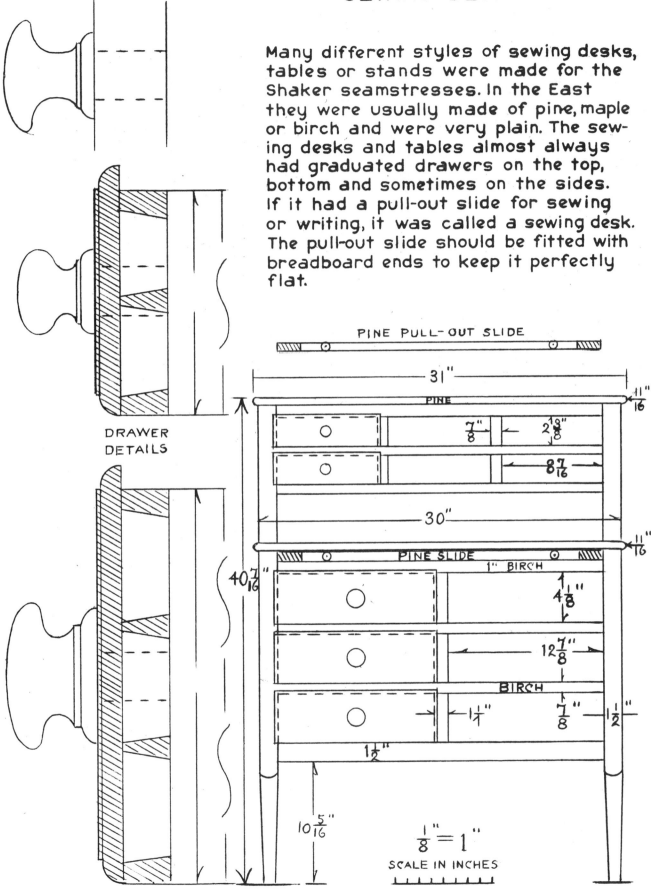

DRAWER DETAILS

PINE PULL-OUT SLIDE

PINE

31"

$\frac{11}{16}$"

$\frac{7}{8}$"    $2\frac{19}{8}$"

$8\frac{7}{16}$"

30"

PINE SLIDE

$\frac{11}{16}$"

1" BIRCH

$4\frac{1}{8}$"

$12\frac{7}{8}$"

$40\frac{7}{16}$"

BIRCH

$1\frac{1}{4}$"    $\frac{7}{8}$"    $1\frac{1}{2}$"

$1\frac{1}{2}$"

$10\frac{5}{16}$"

$\frac{1}{8}$" = 1"

SCALE IN INCHES

12

# SEWING DESK

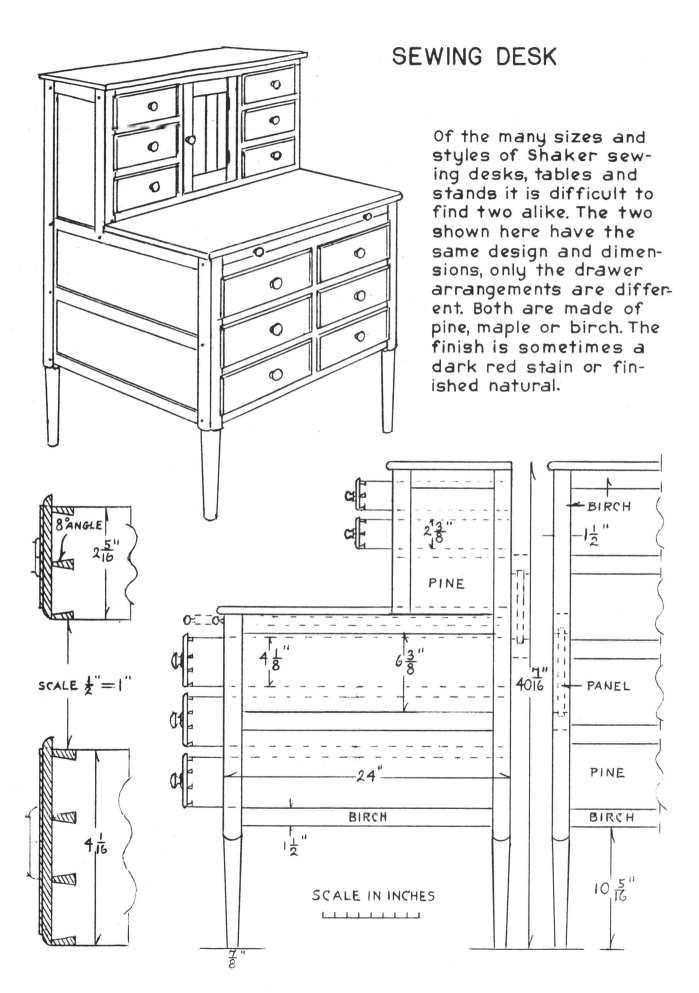

Of the many sizes and styles of Shaker sewing desks, tables and stands it is difficult to find two alike. The two shown here have the same design and dimensions, only the drawer arrangements are different. Both are made of pine, maple or birch. The finish is sometimes a dark red stain or finished natural.

8° ANGLE

$2\frac{5}{16}$"

SCALE $\frac{1}{2}$" = 1"

$4\frac{1}{16}$

$2\frac{3}{8}$"

PINE

BIRCH

$1\frac{1}{2}$"

$4\frac{1}{8}$"

$6\frac{3}{8}$"

$40\frac{7}{16}$"

PANEL

24"

PINE

BIRCH

BIRCH

$1\frac{1}{2}$"

$10\frac{5}{16}$"

$\frac{7}{8}$"

SCALE IN INCHES

# SEWING STAND
## MAPLE

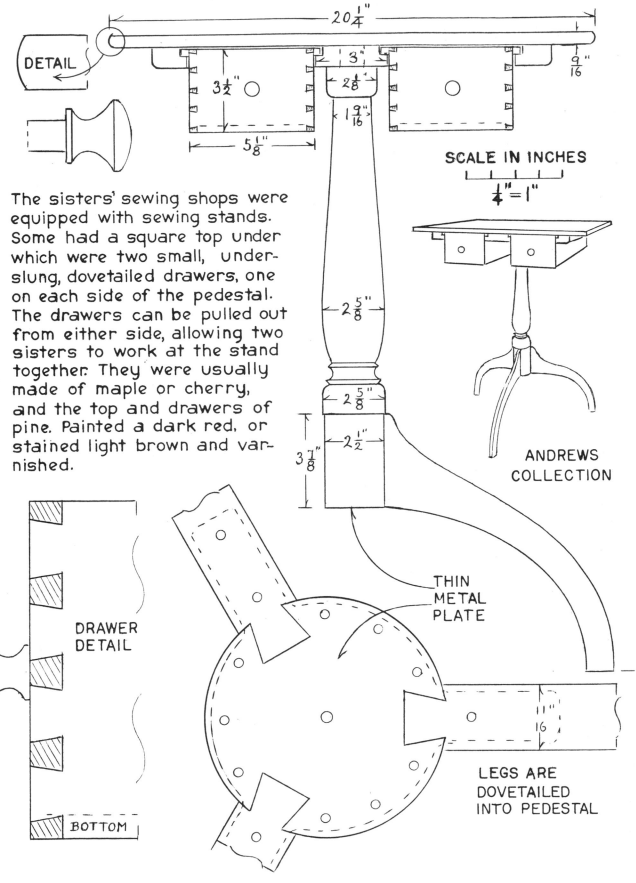

20$\frac{1}{4}$"

DETAIL

3$\frac{1}{2}$"

5$\frac{1}{8}$"

3"

2$\frac{1}{8}$"

1$\frac{9}{16}$"

$\frac{9}{16}$"

2$\frac{5}{8}$"

2$\frac{5}{8}$"

2$\frac{1}{2}$"

3$\frac{7}{8}$"

SCALE IN INCHES

$\frac{1}{4}$"=1"

ANDREWS
COLLECTION

The sisters' sewing shops were equipped with sewing stands. Some had a square top under which were two small, underslung, dovetailed drawers, one on each side of the pedestal. The drawers can be pulled out from either side, allowing two sisters to work at the stand together. They were usually made of maple or cherry, and the top and drawers of pine. Painted a dark red, or stained light brown and varnished.

DRAWER
DETAIL

BOTTOM

THIN
METAL
PLATE

$\frac{11}{16}$"

LEGS ARE
DOVETAILED
INTO PEDESTAL

# WORKSTAND
## OF MAPLE WITH PINE TOP AND DRAWER

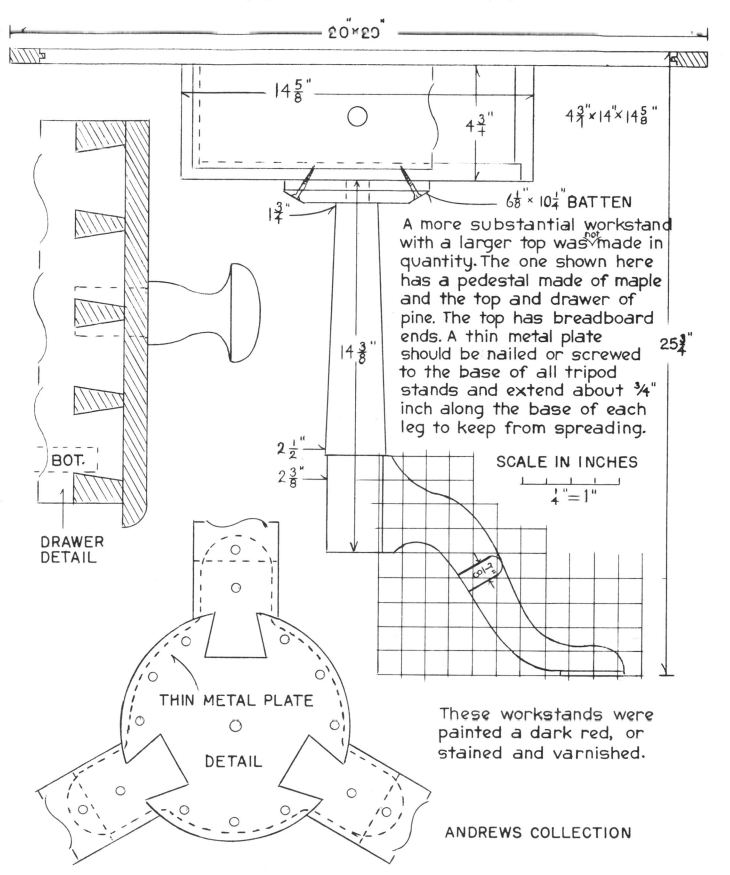

20"×20"

$14\frac{5}{8}$"

$4\frac{3}{4}$"

$4\frac{3}{4}$"×14"×$14\frac{5}{8}$"

$6\frac{1}{8}$"×$10\frac{1}{4}$" BATTEN

$1\frac{3}{4}$"

$14\frac{3}{8}$"

$2\frac{1}{2}$"

$2\frac{3}{8}$"

$25\frac{3}{4}$"

$\frac{5}{16}$"

A more substantial workstand with a larger top was not made in quantity. The one shown here has a pedestal made of maple and the top and drawer of pine. The top has breadboard ends. A thin metal plate should be nailed or screwed to the base of all tripod stands and extend about ¾" inch along the base of each leg to keep from spreading.

SCALE IN INCHES

$\frac{1}{4}$"=1"

BOT.

DRAWER DETAIL

THIN METAL PLATE

DETAIL

These workstands were painted a dark red, or stained and varnished.

ANDREWS COLLECTION

15

# CANDLESTAND
## FROM ANDREWS COLLECTION

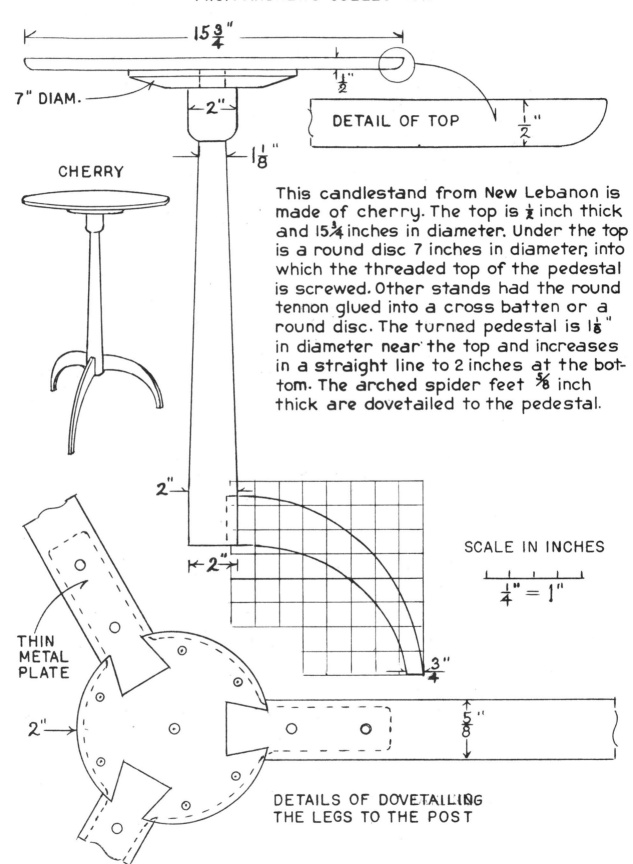

15¾"

7" DIAM.

CHERRY

2"

1½"

DETAIL OF TOP

½"

1⅛"

This candlestand from New Lebanon is made of cherry. The top is ½ inch thick and 15¾ inches in diameter. Under the top is a round disc 7 inches in diameter, into which the threaded top of the pedestal is screwed. Other stands had the round tennon glued into a cross batten or a round disc. The turned pedestal is 1⅛" in diameter near the top and increases in a straight line to 2 inches at the bottom. The arched spider feet ⅝ inch thick are dovetailed to the pedestal.

2"

2"

SCALE IN INCHES

¼" = 1"

THIN METAL PLATE

2"

3" / 4"

5" / 8"

DETAILS OF DOVETAILING THE LEGS TO THE POST

# CANDLESTAND
## PRIVATE COLLECTION

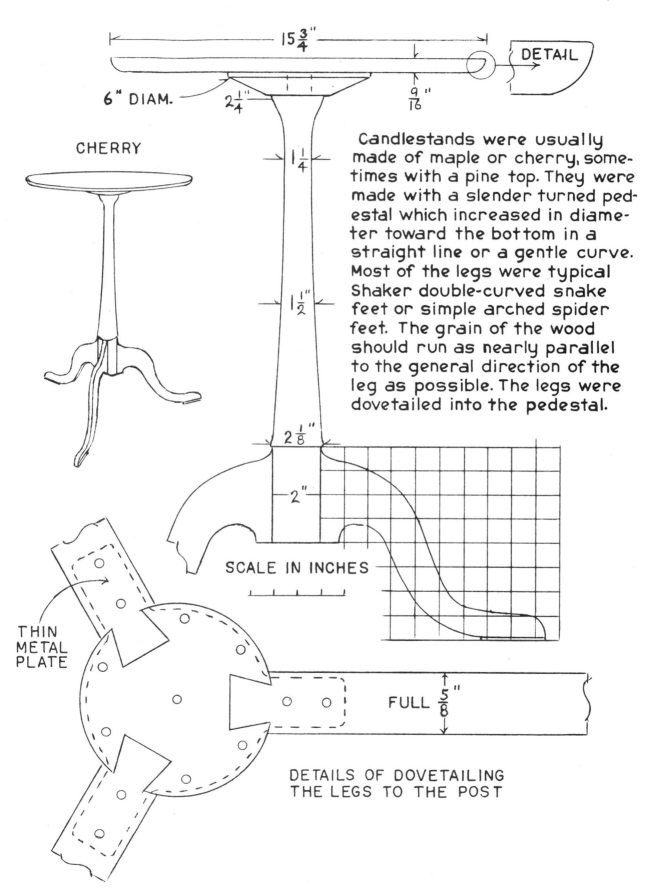

15¾"

DETAIL

6" DIAM.

2¼"

$\frac{9}{16}$"

CHERRY

1¼"

1½"

2⅛"

2"

Candlestands were usually made of maple or cherry, sometimes with a pine top. They were made with a slender turned pedestal which increased in diameter toward the bottom in a straight line or a gentle curve. Most of the legs were typical Shaker double-curved snake feet or simple arched spider feet. The grain of the wood should run as nearly parallel to the general direction of the leg as possible. The legs were dovetailed into the pedestal.

SCALE IN INCHES

THIN METAL PLATE

FULL ⅝"

DETAILS OF DOVETAILING THE LEGS TO THE POST

# TRESTLE TABLE

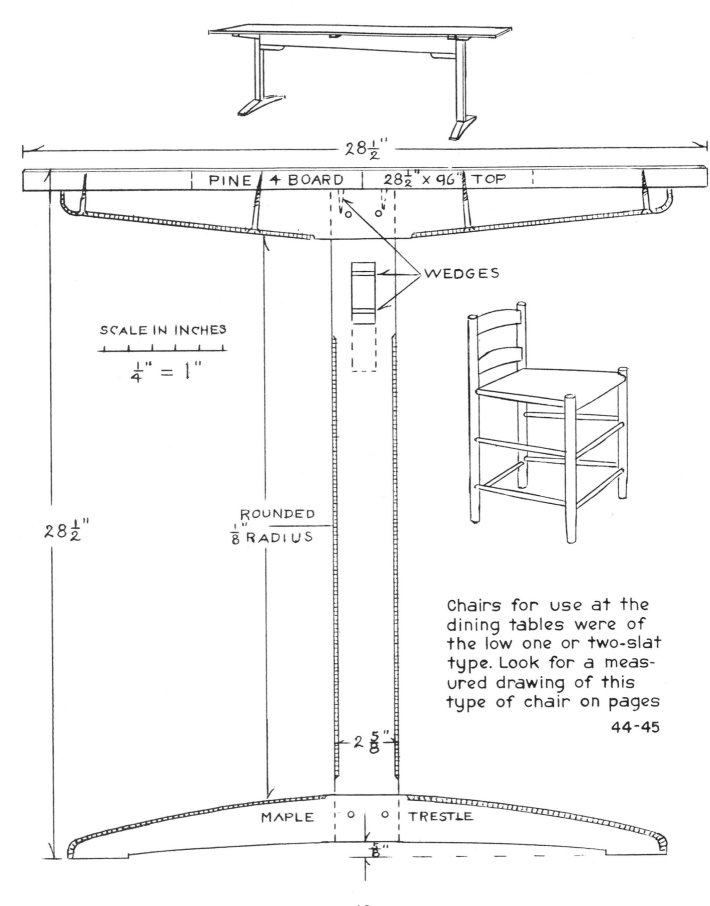

28½"

PINE · 4 BOARD · 28½" x 96" TOP

WEDGES

SCALE IN INCHES

¼" = 1"

ROUNDED
⅛" RADIUS

28½"

Chairs for use at the
dining tables were of
the low one or two-slat
type. Look for a meas-
ured drawing of this
type of chair on pages
44-45

2⅝"

MAPLE · TRESTLE

⅝"

# TRESTLE TABLE

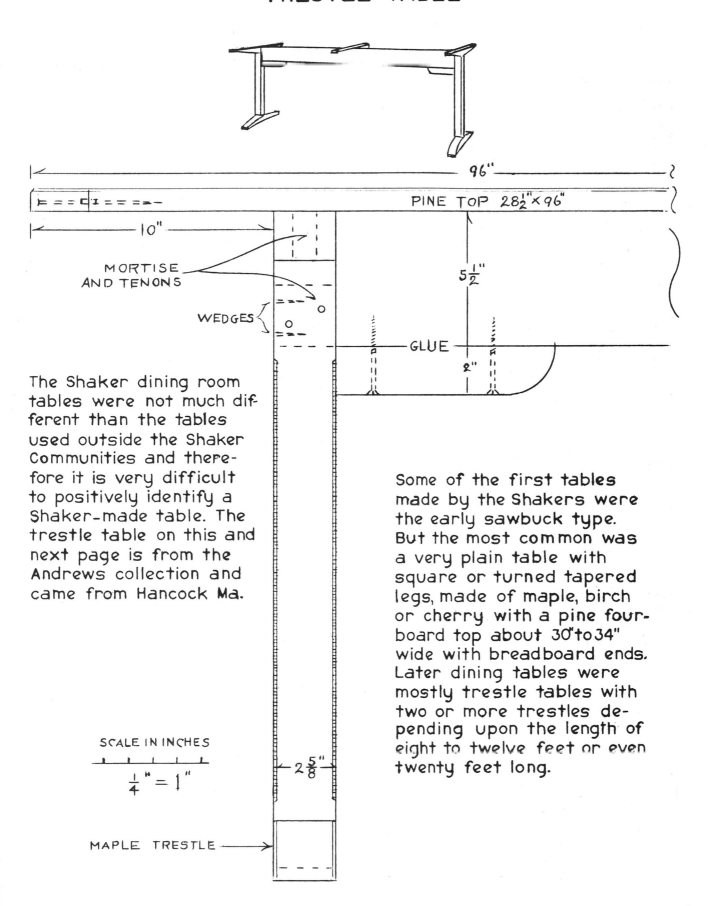

96"

PINE TOP 28½" x 96"

10"

MORTISE AND TENONS

WEDGES

5 ½"

GLUE

2"

The Shaker dining room tables were not much different than the tables used outside the Shaker Communities and therefore it is very difficult to positively identify a Shaker-made table. The trestle table on this and next page is from the Andrews collection and came from Hancock Ma.

Some of the first tables made by the Shakers were the early sawbuck type. But the most common was a very plain table with square or turned tapered legs, made of maple, birch or cherry with a pine four-board top about 30"to34" wide with breadboard ends. Later dining tables were mostly trestle tables with two or more trestles depending upon the length of eight to twelve feet or even twenty feet long.

SCALE IN INCHES

¼" = 1"

2 ⅝"

MAPLE TRESTLE

# LOW WORK TABLE
## PRIVATE COLLECTION

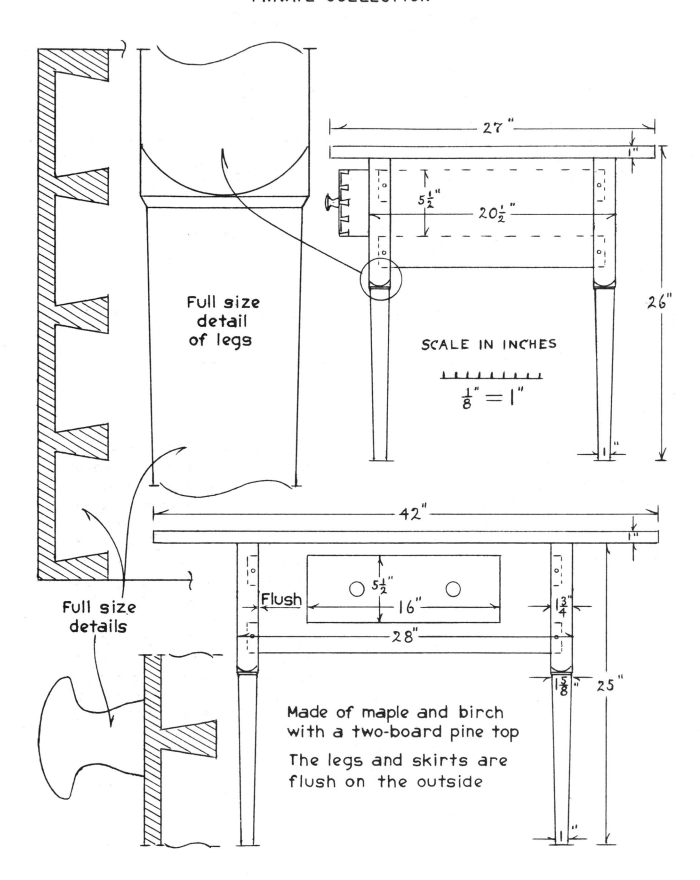

Full size
detail
of legs

27"

1"

5½"

20½"

26"

1"

SCALE IN INCHES

$\frac{1}{8}" = 1"$

Full size
details

42"

1"

Flush

5½"

16"

1¾"

28"

1⅝"

25"

1"

Made of maple and birch
with a two-board pine top

The legs and skirts are
flush on the outside

# TABLE WITH SPLAYED LEGS
## FROM MT. LEBANON, N.Y. CA. 1835
### CHARLES L. FLINT, ANTIQUES, LENOX, MASS.

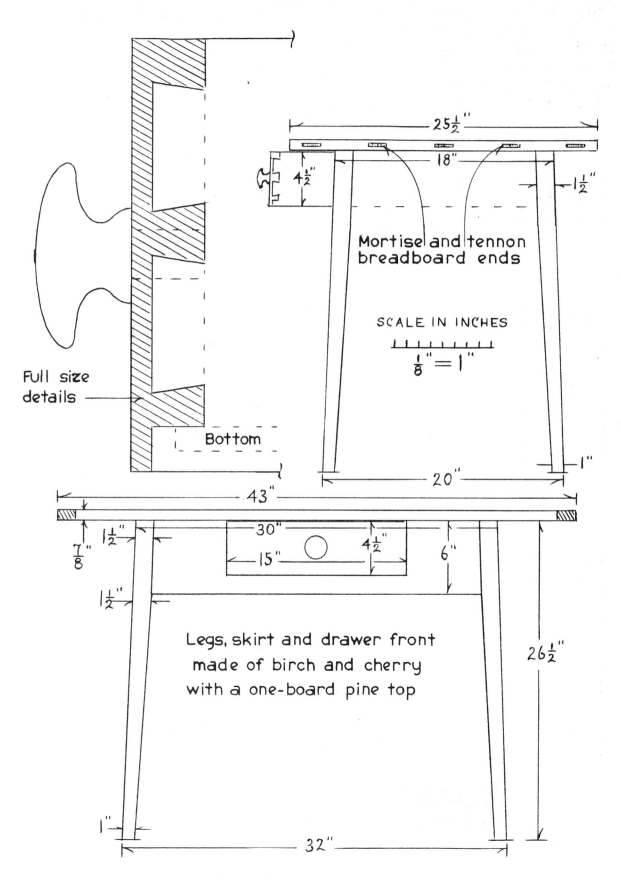

Full size details

Bottom

$25\frac{1}{2}$"

18"

$4\frac{1}{2}$"

$1\frac{1}{2}$"

Mortise and tennon breadboard ends

SCALE IN INCHES

$\frac{1}{8}$" = 1"

20"

1"

43"

$1\frac{1}{2}$"

$\frac{7}{8}$"

30"

15"

$4\frac{1}{2}$"

6"

$1\frac{1}{2}$"

Legs, skirt and drawer front made of birch and cherry with a one-board pine top

$26\frac{1}{2}$"

1"

32"

Drop-leaf tables were usually made of cherry or maple. The longer ones, up to eight ft. in length, were used in the kitchen, dining room and as workroom tables. But others not much over 30 inches in length were used in the retiring rooms. The leaves, from 6 to 8 inches wide were supported by two wood strips pulled out by small wooden knobs from the top of the table frame.

# DROP-LEAF TABLE
## CHERRY

PRIVATE COLLECTION

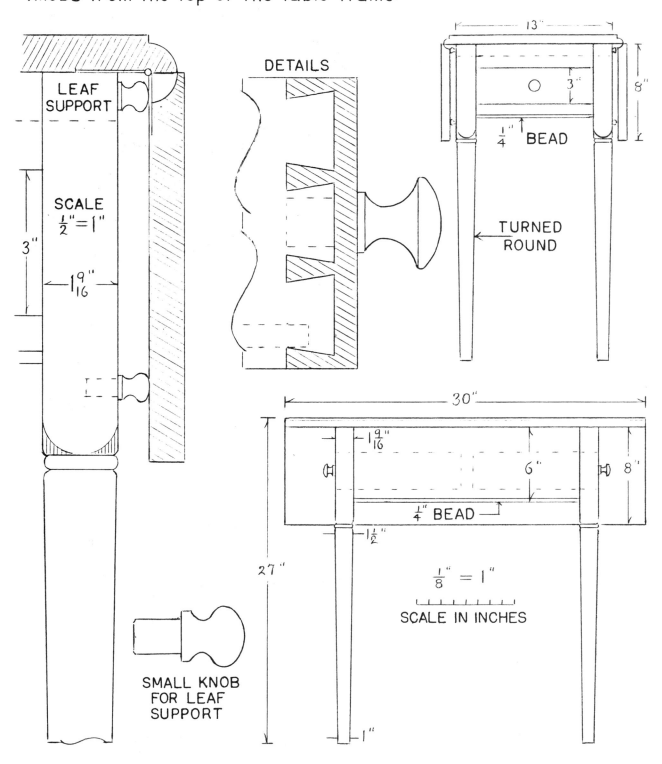

LEAF SUPPORT

DETAILS

SCALE
$\frac{1}{2}" = 1"$

3"

$1\frac{9}{16}"$

13"

8"

$\frac{1}{4}"$ BEAD

3"

TURNED ROUND

30"

$1\frac{9}{16}"$

6"

8"

$\frac{1}{4}"$ BEAD

$1\frac{1}{2}"$

27"

$\frac{1}{8}" = 1"$

SCALE IN INCHES

1"

SMALL KNOB FOR LEAF SUPPORT

Some drop-leaf tables have only one leaf, on the side to the wall. The other side has one or two long and shallow drawers. The legs were either square tapered or turned, beginning with a small collar and tapering from about 1½ inches in diameter to about 1 inch at the floor.

# DROP-LEAF TABLE
## MAPLE

### PRIVATE COLLECTION

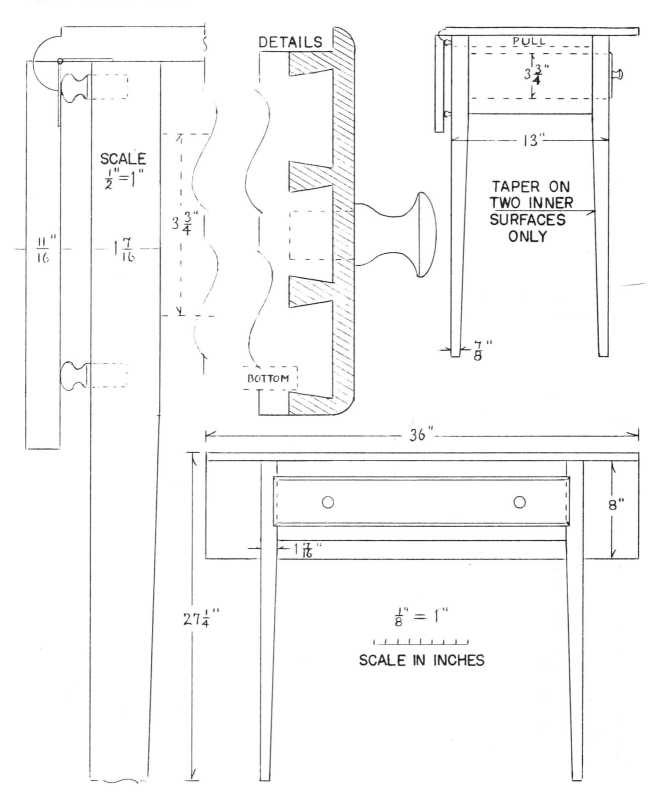

DETAILS

SCALE ½" = 1"

$\frac{11}{16}$"

$1\frac{7}{16}$

$3\frac{3}{4}$

BOTTOM

PULL

$3\frac{3}{4}$"

13"

TAPER ON TWO INNER SURFACES ONLY

$\frac{7}{8}$"

36"

8"

$1\frac{7}{16}$"

$27\frac{1}{4}$"

⅛" = 1"

SCALE IN INCHES

23

# PINE WASHSTAND
## NEW LEBANON N.Y.

## MUSEUM OF FINE ARTS, BOSTON, MASS.

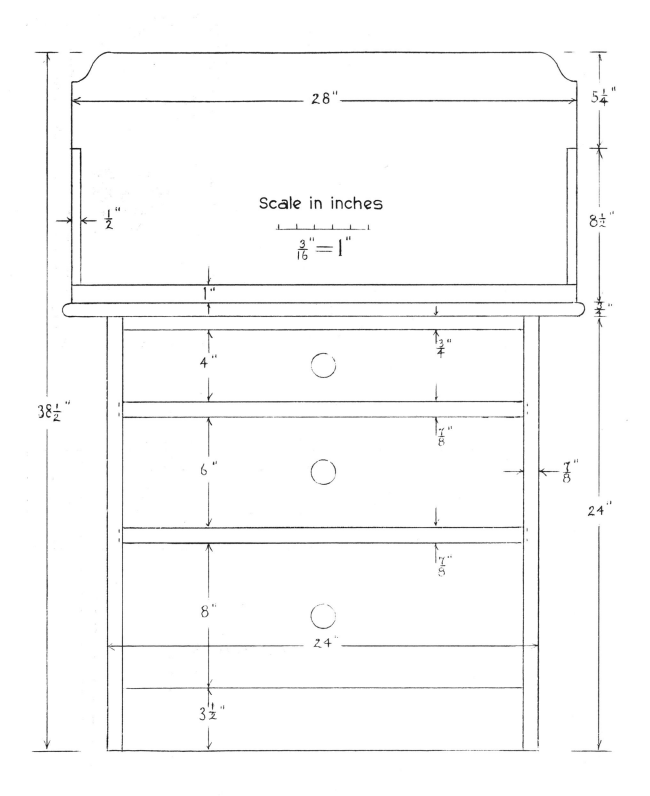

Scale in inches

$\frac{3}{16}" = 1"$

# PINE WASHSTAND
## NEW LEBANON N.Y.

## MUSEUM OF FINE ARTS, BOSTON, MASS.

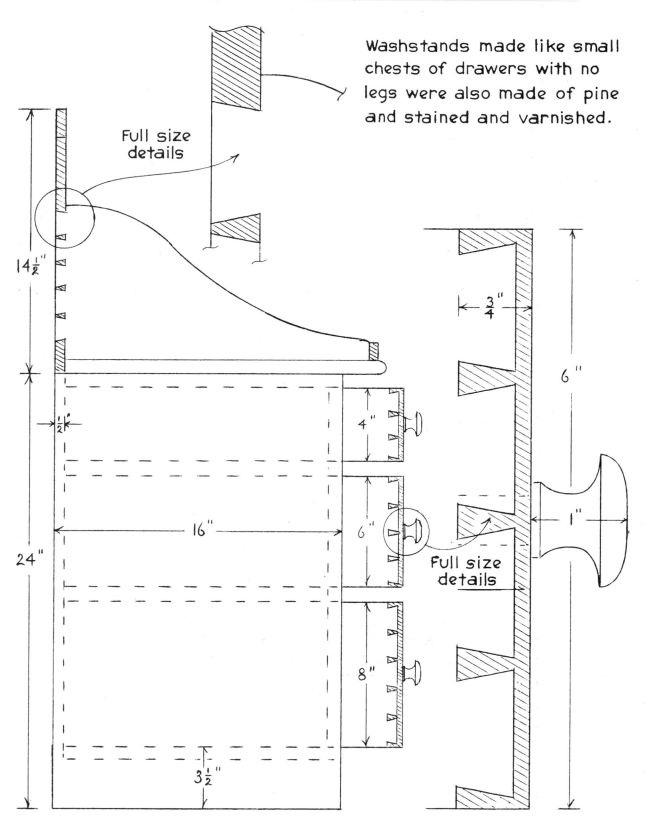

Washstands made like small
chests of drawers with no
legs were also made of pine
and stained and varnished.

Full size
details

Full size
details

$14\frac{1}{2}''$

$\frac{1}{2}''$

$16''$

$24''$

$3\frac{1}{2}''$

$4''$

$6''$

$8''$

$\frac{3}{4}''$

$6''$

$1''$

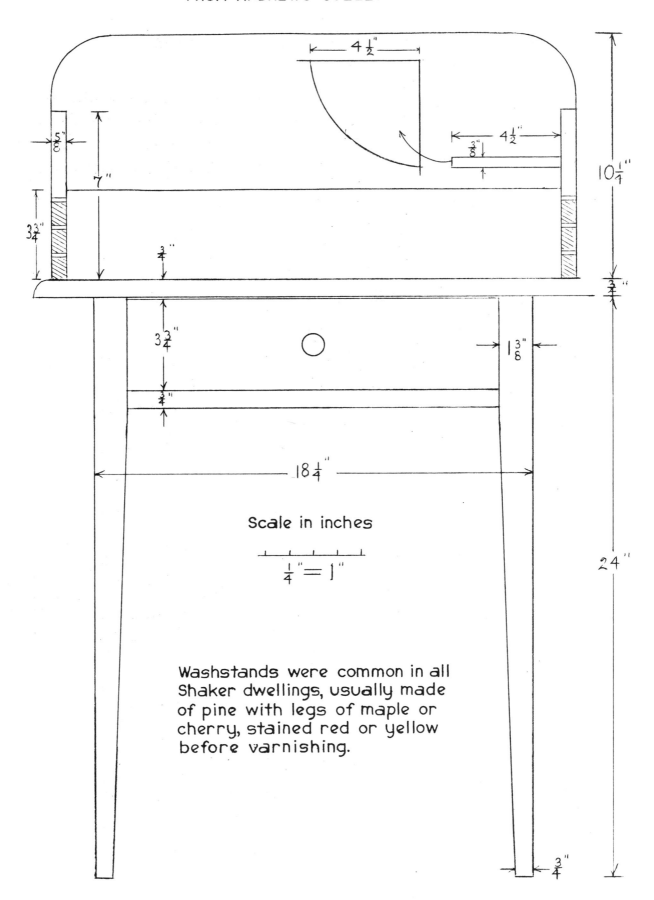

Scale in inches

$\frac{1}{4}" = 1"$

Washstands were common in all
Shaker dwellings, usually made
of pine with legs of maple or
cherry, stained red or yellow
before varnishing.

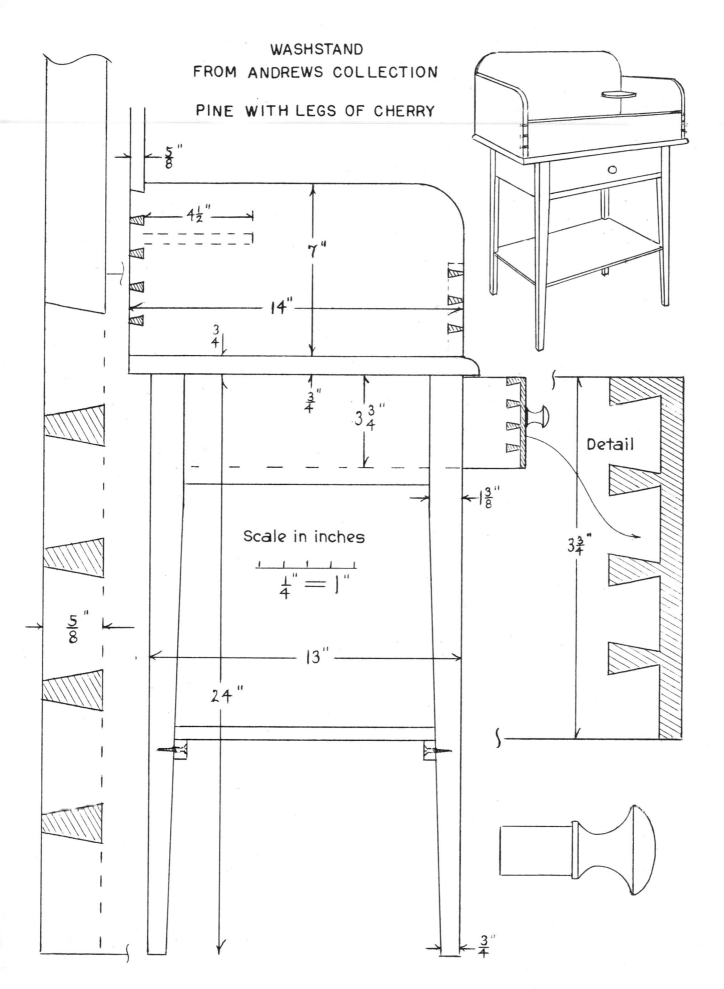

WASHSTAND
FROM ANDREWS COLLECTION

PINE WITH LEGS OF CHERRY

$\frac{5}{8}$"

$4\frac{1}{2}$"

7"

14"

$\frac{3}{4}$

$\frac{3}{4}$"

$3\frac{3}{4}$"

$1\frac{3}{8}$"

Detail

$3\frac{3}{4}$"

Scale in inches

$\frac{1}{4}$" = 1"

13"

$\frac{5}{8}$"

24"

$\frac{3}{4}$"

# WOOD-BOX
## PINE, STAINED RED.

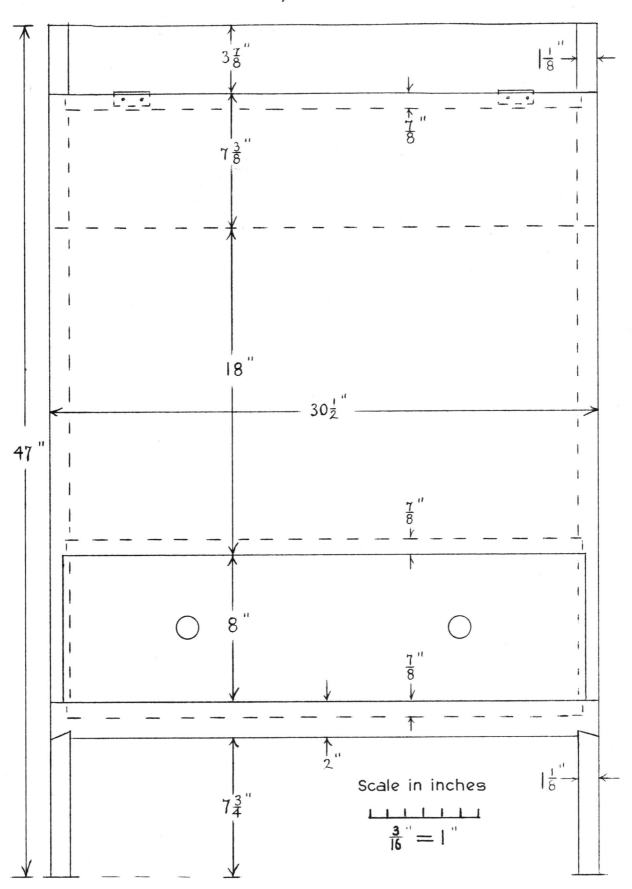

Scale in inches

$\frac{3}{16}'' = 1''$

28

# WOOD-BOX
## PINE, STAINED RED.

### FROM
### ANDREWS COLLECTION.

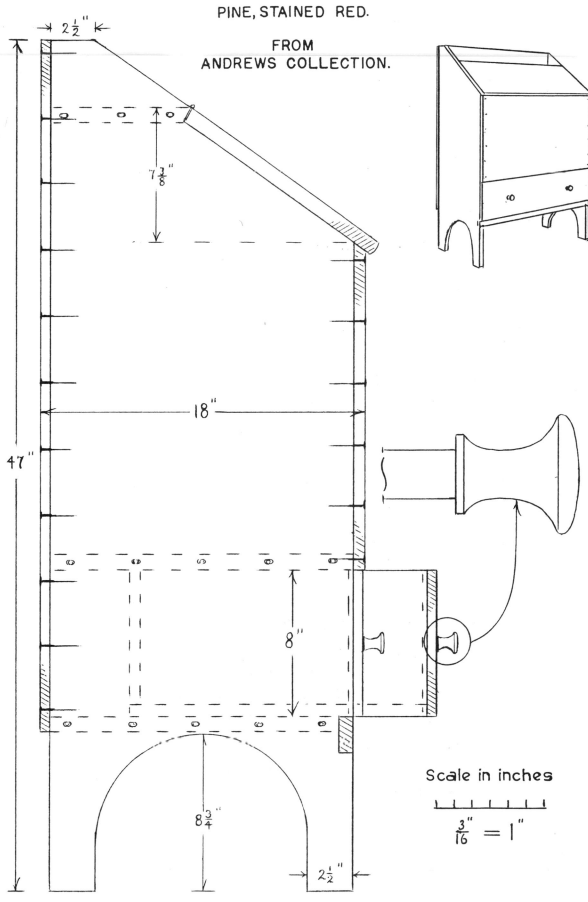

$2\frac{1}{2}$"

$7\frac{1}{8}$"

47"

18"

8"

$8\frac{3}{4}$"

$2\frac{1}{2}$"

Scale in inches

$\frac{3}{16}$" = 1"

29

# WOOD-BOX

## PLEASANT HILL KENTUCKY.

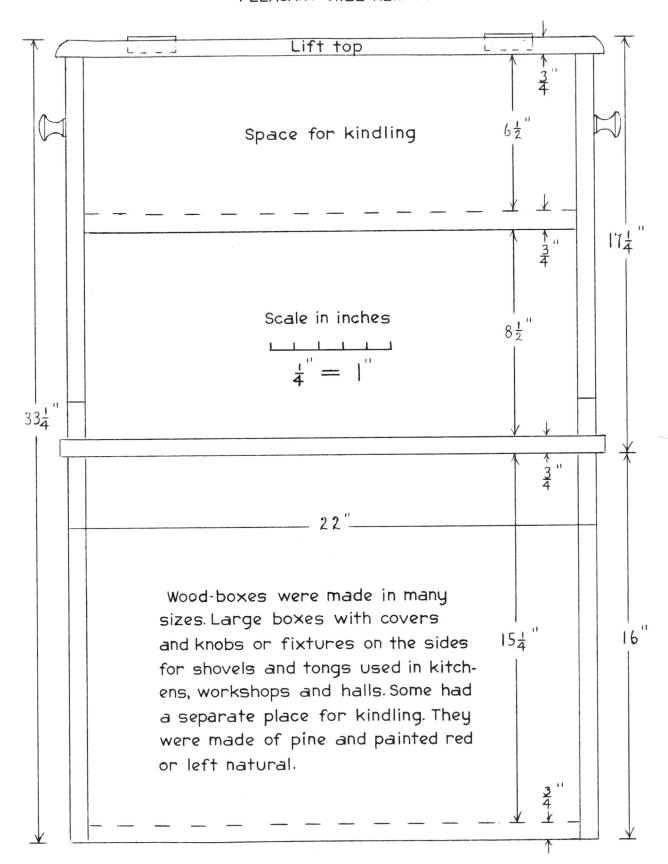

Lift top

Space for kindling

$\frac{3}{4}$"

$6\frac{1}{2}$"

$17\frac{1}{4}$"

Scale in inches

$\frac{1}{4}$" = 1"

$\frac{3}{4}$"

$8\frac{1}{2}$"

$33\frac{1}{4}$"

$\frac{3}{4}$"

22"

$15\frac{1}{4}$"

16"

Wood-boxes were made in many
sizes. Large boxes with covers
and knobs or fixtures on the sides
for shovels and tongs used in kitch-
ens, workshops and halls. Some had
a separate place for kindling. They
were made of pine and painted red
or left natural.

$\frac{3}{4}$"

# WOOD BOX
## PLEASANT HILL, KENTUCKY.

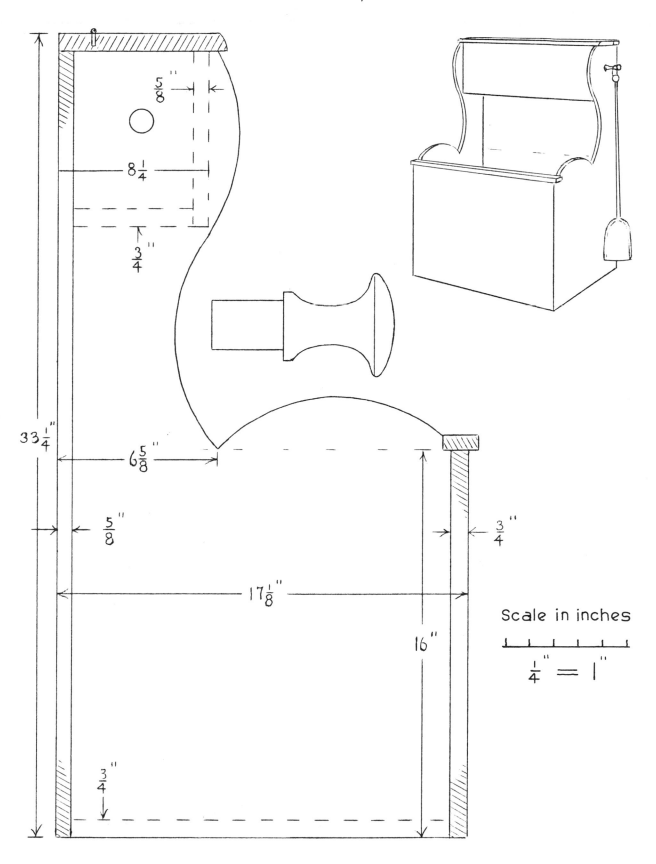

Scale in inches

$\frac{1}{4}'' = 1''$

## The Shakers' Web Back Chairs, with Arms and Rockers.

WORSTED LACE SEATS AND BACKS.

Showing a Comparison of Sizes.

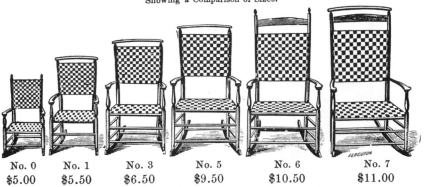

| No. 0 | No. 1 | No. 3 | No. 5 | No. 6 | No. 7 |
|-------|-------|-------|-------|-------|-------|
| $5.00 | $5.50 | $6.50 | $9.50 | $10.50 | $11.00 |

## The Shakers' Web Back Chairs, With Rockers.

WORSTED LACE SEATS AND BACKS.

Showing a Comparison of Sizes.

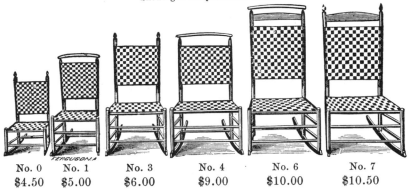

| No. 0 | No. 1 | No. 3 | No. 4 | No. 6 | No. 7 |
|-------|-------|-------|-------|-------|-------|
| $4.50 | $5.00 | $6.00 | $9.00 | $10.00 | $10.50 |

## The Shakers' Slat Back Chairs, with Arms and Rockers.

WORSTED LACE SEATS.

Showing a Comparison of Sizes.

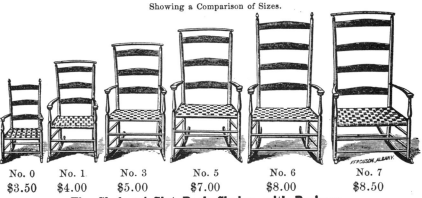

| No. 0 | No. 1 | No. 3 | No. 5 | No. 6 | No. 7 |
|-------|-------|-------|-------|-------|-------|
| $3.50 | $4.00 | $5.00 | $7.00 | $8.00 | $8.50 |

## The Shakers' Slat Back Chairs, with Rockers.

WORSTED LACE SEATS.

Showing a Comparison of Sizes.

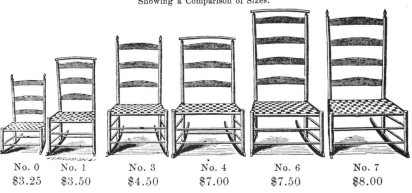

| No. 0 | No. 1 | No. 3 | No. 4 | No. 6 | No. 7 |
|-------|-------|-------|-------|-------|-------|
| $3.25 | $3.50 | $4.50 | $7.00 | $7.50 | $8.00 |

# MT. LEBANON CHAIRS.

The following quotations and the descriptions on the Plates are taken from a Shaker chair catalog dated 1876:

" . . . a description and a representation of the different sizes of chairs and foot benches which we manufacture and sell. We would also call attention of the public to the fact that there is no other chair manufactory which is owned and operated by the Shakers, except the one which is now in operation and owned and operated by the Society of Shakers, at Mount Lebanon, Columbia, county, N.Y. We deem it a duty we owe the public to enlighten them in this matter, owing to the fact that there are now several manufacturers of chairs who have made and introduced into market an imitation of our own styles of chairs, which they sell for Shakers' Chairs, and which are unquestionably bought by the public generally under the impression that they are the real genuine article, made by the Shakers at their establishment in Mount Lebanon, N.Y. Of all the imitations of our chairs which have come under our observation, there is none which we would be willing to accept as our workmanship, nor would we be willing to stake our reputation on their merits.

"The increasing demand for our chairs has prompted us to increase the facilities for producing and improving them. We have spared no expense or labor in our endeavors to produce an article that cannot be surpassed in any respect, and which combines all the advantages of durability, simplicity and lightness.

"The bars across the top of back posts are intended for cushions, but will be furnished to order without additional cost.

"Many of our friends who see the Shakers' chairs for the first time may be led to suppose that the chair business is a new thing for the Shakers to engage in. This is not the fact, however, and may surprise even some of the oldest manufacturers to learn that the Shakers were pioneers in the business after the establishment of the independence of the country.

"The principles as well as the rules of the Society forbid the trustees or any of their assistants doing business on the credit system, either in the purchase or sale of merchandise, or making bargains or contracts. This we consider good policy, and a safe way of doing business, checking speculative or dishonest propensities, and averting financial panics and disasters. We sell with the understanding that all bills are to be cash.

"Look for our trade-mark before purchasing—no chair is genuine without it. Our trade-mark is a gold transfer, and is designed to be ornamental; but, if objectionable to purchasers, it can be easily removed without defacing the furniture in the least, by wetting a sponge or piece of cotton cloth with AQUA AMMONIA, and rubbing it until it is loosened."

☞We were awarded a Diploma and Medal at the Centennial Exhibition for combining in our Chairs, Strength, Sprightliness and Modest Beauty.

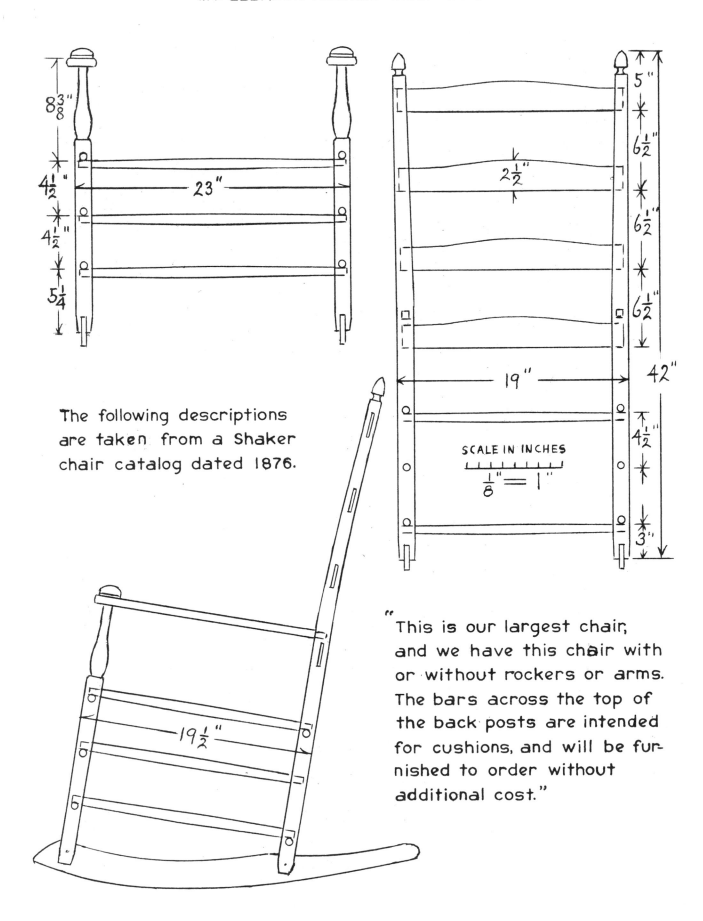

The following descriptions
are taken from a Shaker
chair catalog dated 1876.

SCALE IN INCHES

$\frac{1}{8}" = 1"$

"This is our largest chair,
and we have this chair with
or without rockers or arms.
The bars across the top of
the back posts are intended
for cushions, and will be furnished to order without
additional cost."

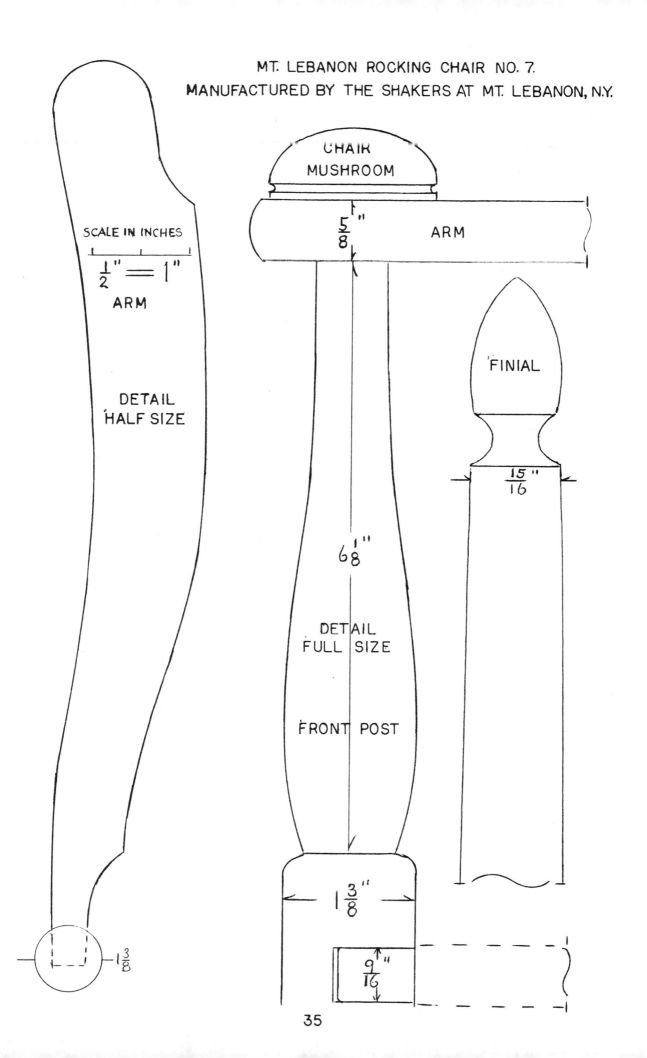

MT. LEBANON ROCKING CHAIR NO. 7.
MANUFACTURED BY THE SHAKERS AT MT. LEBANON, N.Y.

CHAIR
MUSHROOM

SCALE IN INCHES

$\frac{1}{2}" = 1"$

ARM

ARM

$\frac{5}{8}"$

DETAIL
HALF SIZE

FINIAL

$\frac{15}{16}"$

$6\frac{1}{8}"$

DETAIL
FULL SIZE

FRONT POST

$1\frac{3}{8}"$

$1\frac{3}{8}$

$\frac{9}{16}"$

MT. LEBANON ROCKING CHAIR NO. 4,
THE SHAKER MUSEUM, OLD CHATHAM, N.Y.

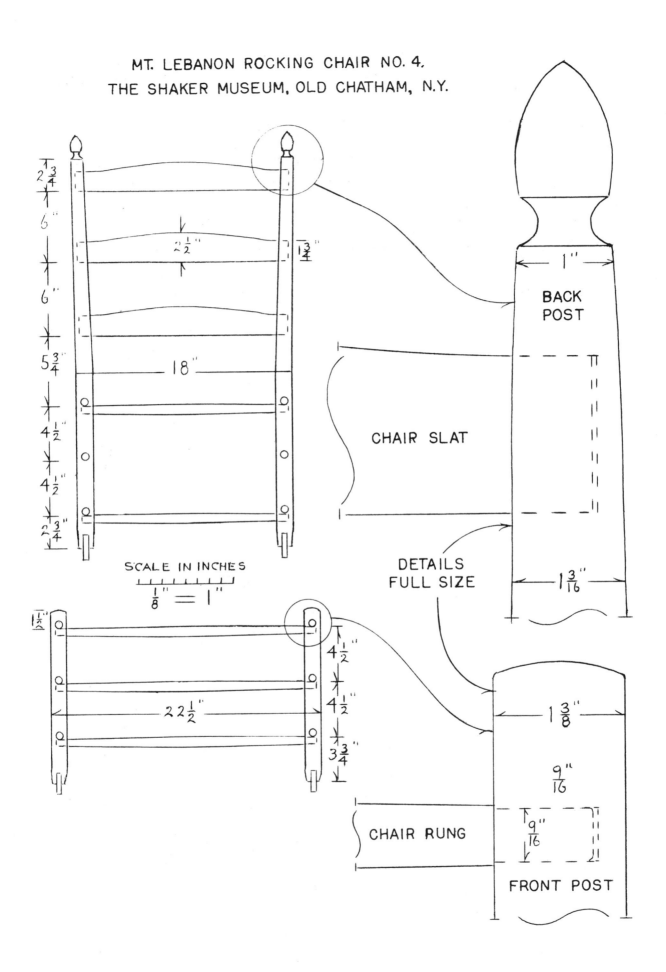

BACK POST

CHAIR SLAT

DETAILS FULL SIZE

$2\frac{3}{4}$

6"

6"

$5\frac{3}{4}$

$4\frac{1}{2}$"

$4\frac{1}{2}$"

$2\frac{3}{4}$"

$2\frac{1}{2}$"

$1\frac{3}{4}$"

18"

1"

$1\frac{3}{16}$"

SCALE IN INCHES

$\frac{1}{8}$" = 1"

$1\frac{1}{2}$"

$22\frac{1}{2}$"

$4\frac{1}{2}$"

$4\frac{1}{2}$"

$3\frac{3}{4}$"

$1\frac{3}{8}$"

$\frac{9}{16}$"

$\frac{9}{16}$"

CHAIR RUNG

FRONT POST

## MT. LEBANON ROCKING CHAIR NO. 4.

"
This chair is a great favorite as
a sewing chair. It is sometimes
made with two drawers under
the seat. Those who want a very
comfortable chair can order with a
web back for only a small additional cost over the slat back."

"
We do not make this size
with arms but have them
with or without rockers"

"
The bars across the top
of the back posts are in-
tended for cushions and
will be furnished to order
without additional cost."

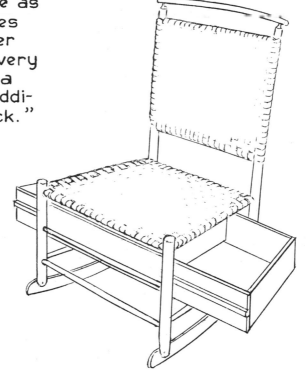

MT. LEBANON ROCKING CHAIR NO. 4.

THE SHAKER MUSEUM,
OLD CHATHAM, N.Y.

CUSHION RAIL

SCALE IN INCHES

$\frac{1}{8}" = 1"$

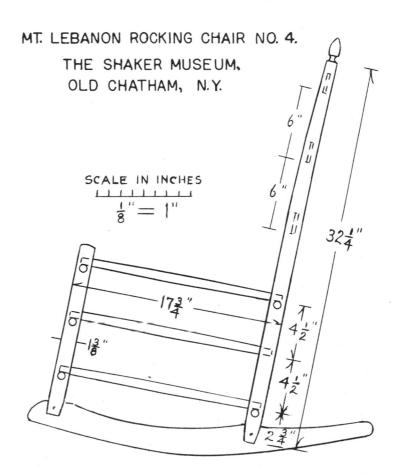

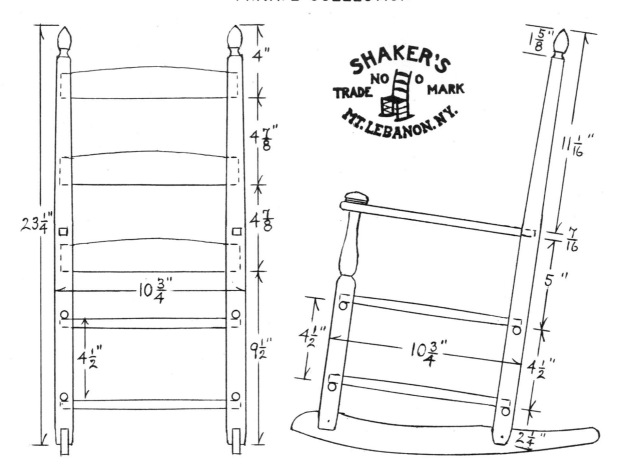

The seven different sizes
of Mt. Lebanon chairs are
made of maple and birch.

SCALE IN INCHES

$\frac{3}{16}$" = 1"

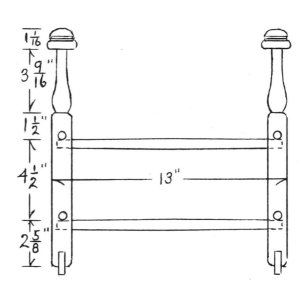

"
This is the smallest size
chair which we make, adapted
to children three or four
years of age or less. We
make this chair with arms
and with or without rockers."

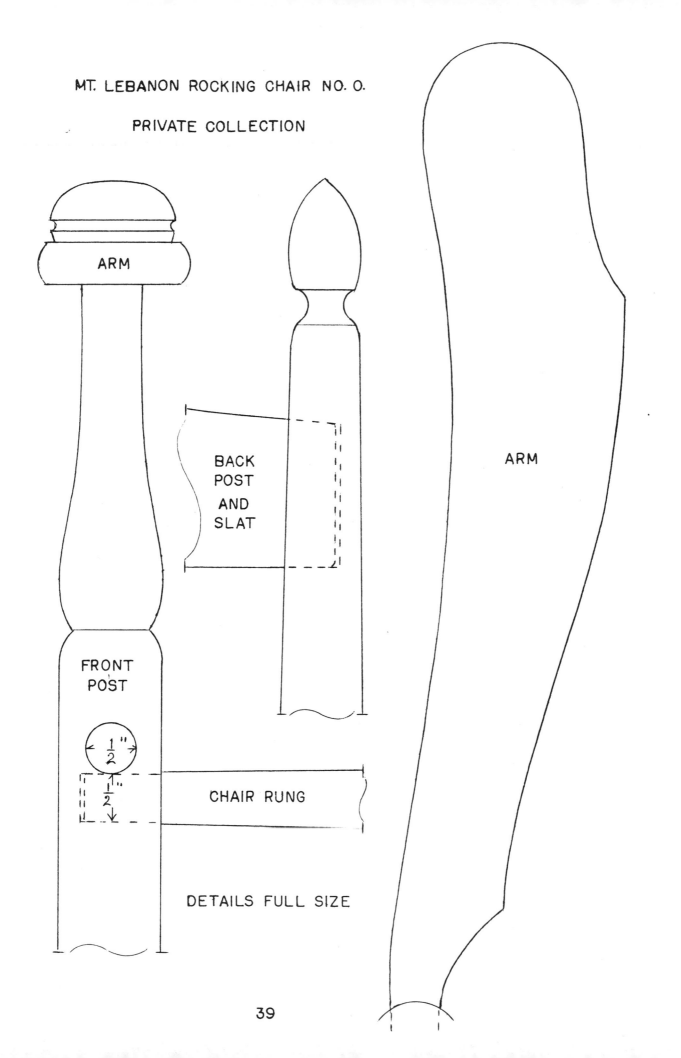

MT. LEBANON ROCKING CHAIR NO. O.

PRIVATE COLLECTION

ARM

BACK
POST
AND
SLAT

ARM

FRONT
POST

$\frac{1}{2}$"

CHAIR RUNG

$\frac{1}{2}$"

DETAILS FULL SIZE

39

# MT. LEBANON ARMCHAIR

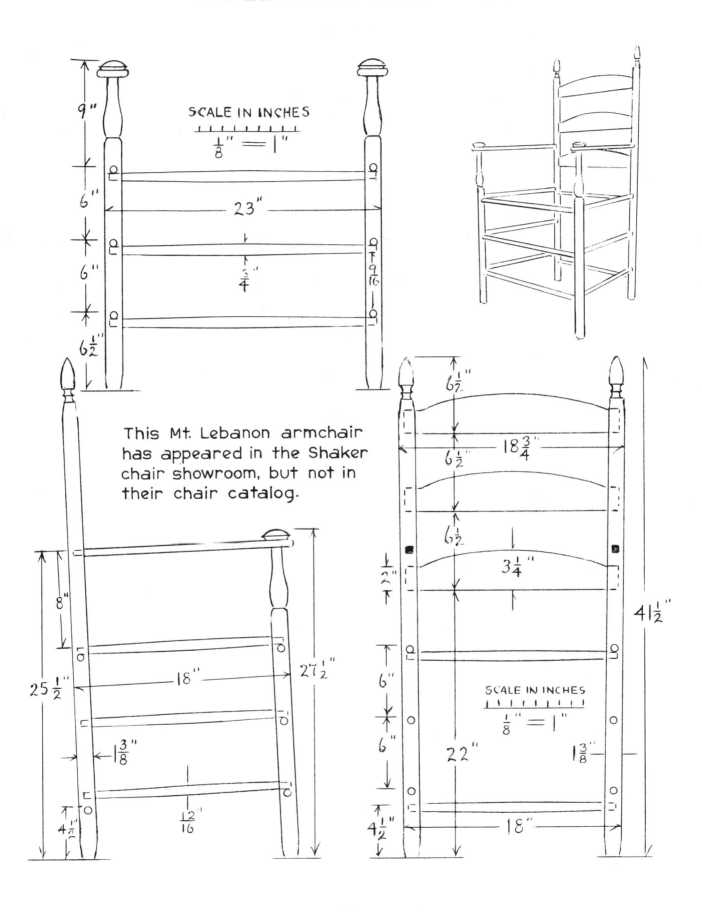

SCALE IN INCHES
$\frac{1}{8}" = 1"$

9"

6"

6"

6½"

23"

¾"

This Mt. Lebanon armchair has appeared in the Shaker chair showroom, but not in their chair catalog.

8"

25½"

18"

27½"

1⅜"

2/16"

6½"

18¾"

6½"

6½"

3¼"

½"

41½"

6"

6"

22"

SCALE IN INCHES
$\frac{1}{8}" = 1"$

1⅜"

4½"

18"

40

# MT. LEBANON ARMCHAIR

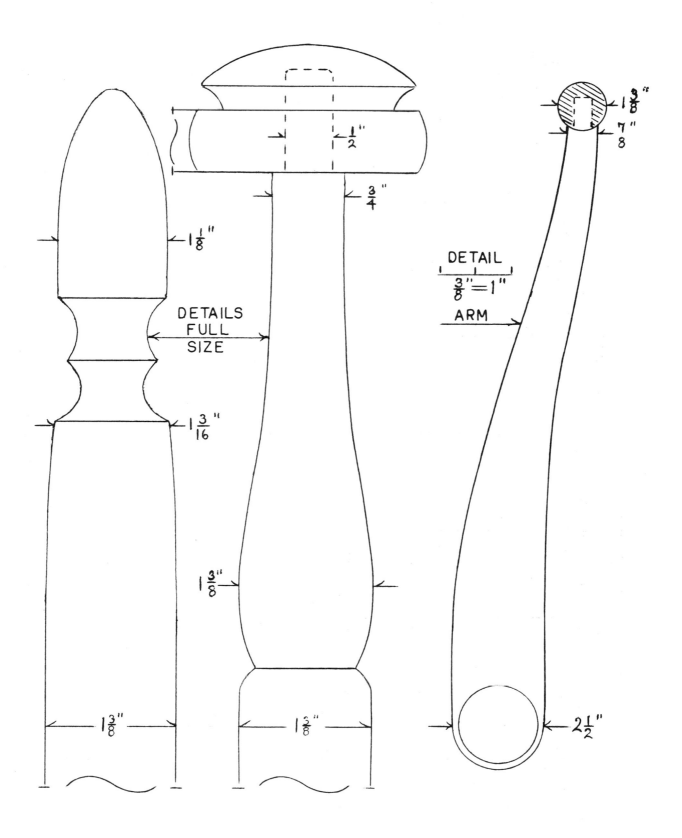

DETAILS FULL SIZE

$1\frac{1}{8}$"

$1\frac{3}{16}$"

$1\frac{3}{8}$"

$\frac{1}{2}$"

$\frac{3}{4}$"

$1\frac{3}{8}$"

$1\frac{3}{8}$"

DETAIL

$\frac{3}{8}$"=1"

ARM

$1\frac{3}{8}$"

$\frac{7}{8}$"

$2\frac{1}{2}$"

# HANCOCK ARMCHAIR

Making chairs to sell was practiced in other Shaker societies, like the Hancock chair makers who were using a peculiarly different finial turning.

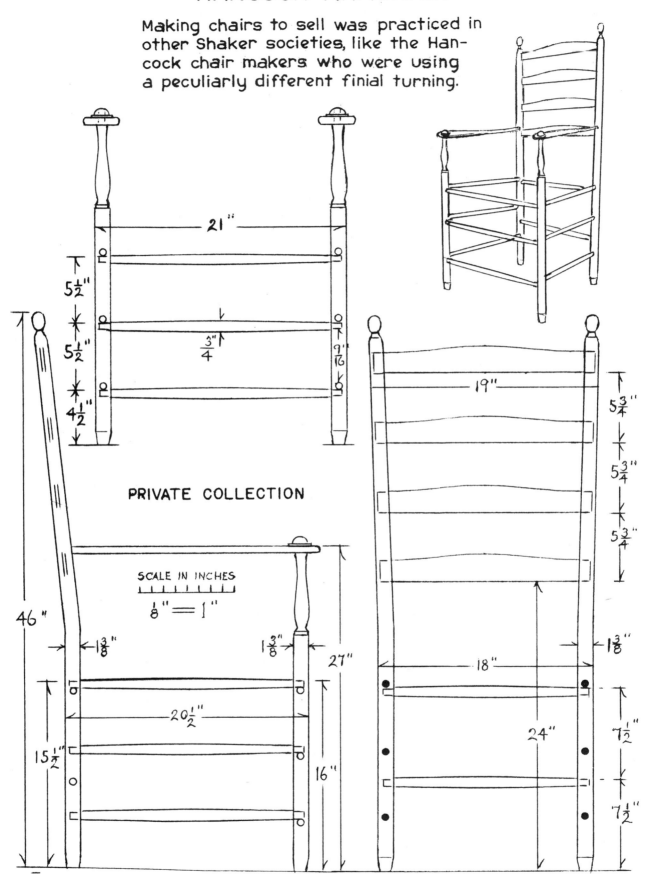

21"

5½"

5½"

4½"

¾"

9/16"

PRIVATE COLLECTION

46"

1⅜"

1⅜"

27"

SCALE IN INCHES

⅛" = 1"

20½"

15½"

16"

19"

5¾"

5¾"

5¾"

18"

1⅜"

1⅜"

24"

7½"

7½"

# HANCOCK ARMCHAIR

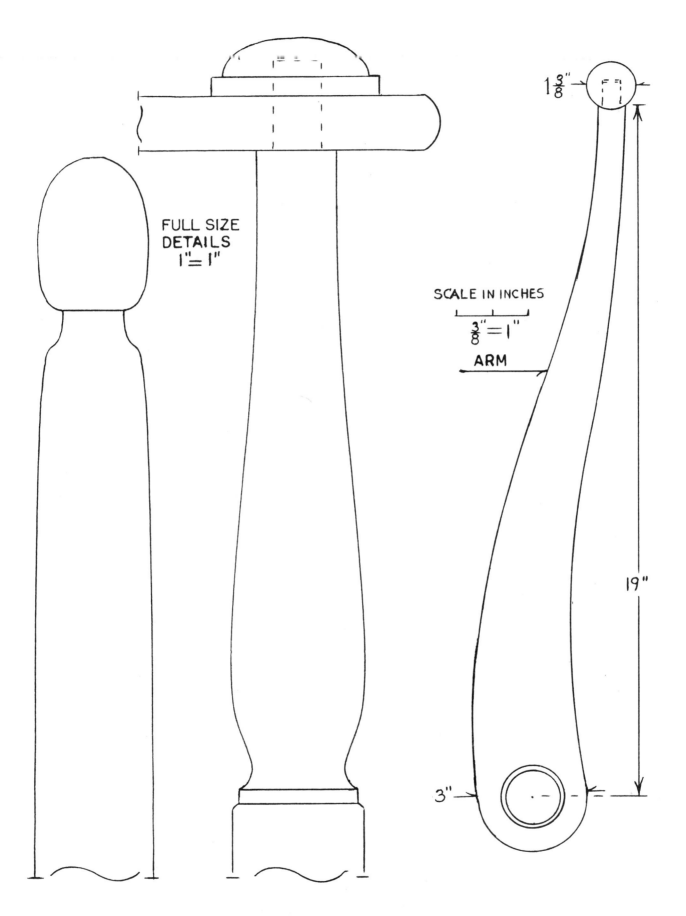

FULL SIZE
DETAILS
1"= 1"

SCALE IN INCHES

$\frac{3}{8}$"= 1"

ARM

$1\frac{3}{8}$"

19"

3"

43

# TWO-SLAT DINING CHAIR

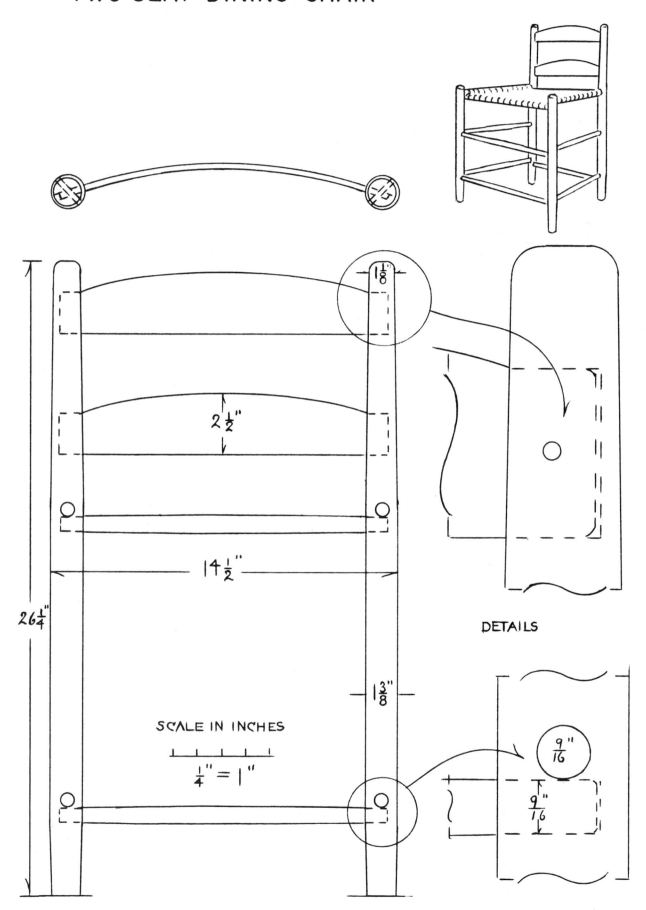

$1\frac{1}{8}$"

$2\frac{1}{2}$"

$14\frac{1}{2}$"

$26\frac{1}{4}$"

DETAILS

$1\frac{3}{8}$"

SCALE IN INCHES

$\frac{1}{4}$" = 1"

$\frac{9}{16}$"

$\frac{9}{16}$"

# TWO-SLAT DINING CHAIR

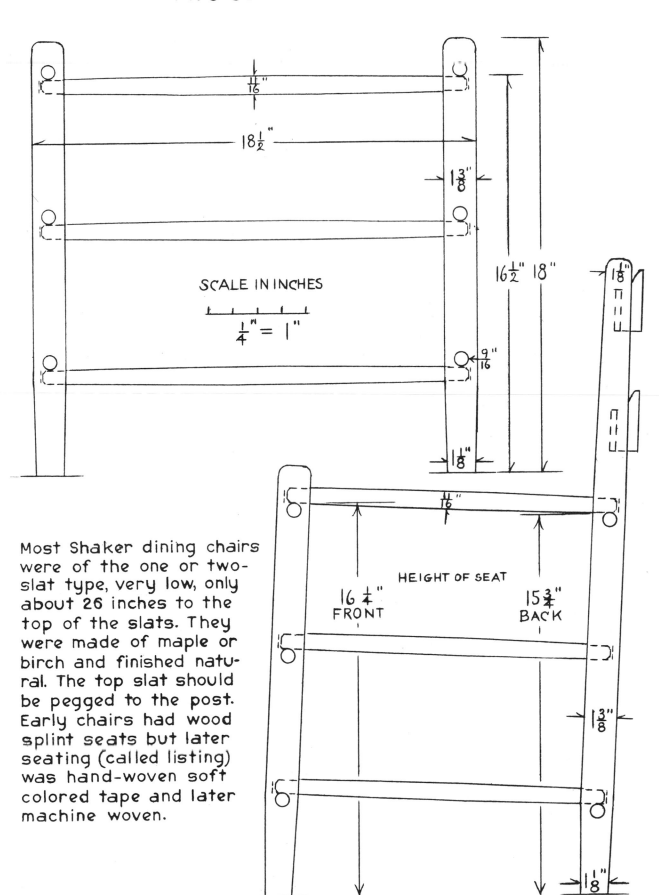

SCALE IN INCHES

$\frac{1}{4}$" = 1"

$\frac{1}{16}$"

18$\frac{1}{2}$"

1$\frac{3}{8}$"

16$\frac{1}{2}$" 18"

$\frac{9}{16}$"

1$\frac{1}{8}$"

1$\frac{1}{8}$"

$\frac{1}{16}$"

HEIGHT OF SEAT

16$\frac{1}{4}$"
FRONT

15$\frac{3}{4}$"
BACK

1$\frac{3}{8}$"

1$\frac{1}{8}$"

Most Shaker dining chairs were of the one or two-slat type, very low, only about 26 inches to the top of the slats. They were made of maple or birch and finished natural. The top slat should be pegged to the post. Early chairs had wood splint seats but later seating (called listing) was hand-woven soft colored tape and later machine woven.

45

# SWIVEL CHAIR

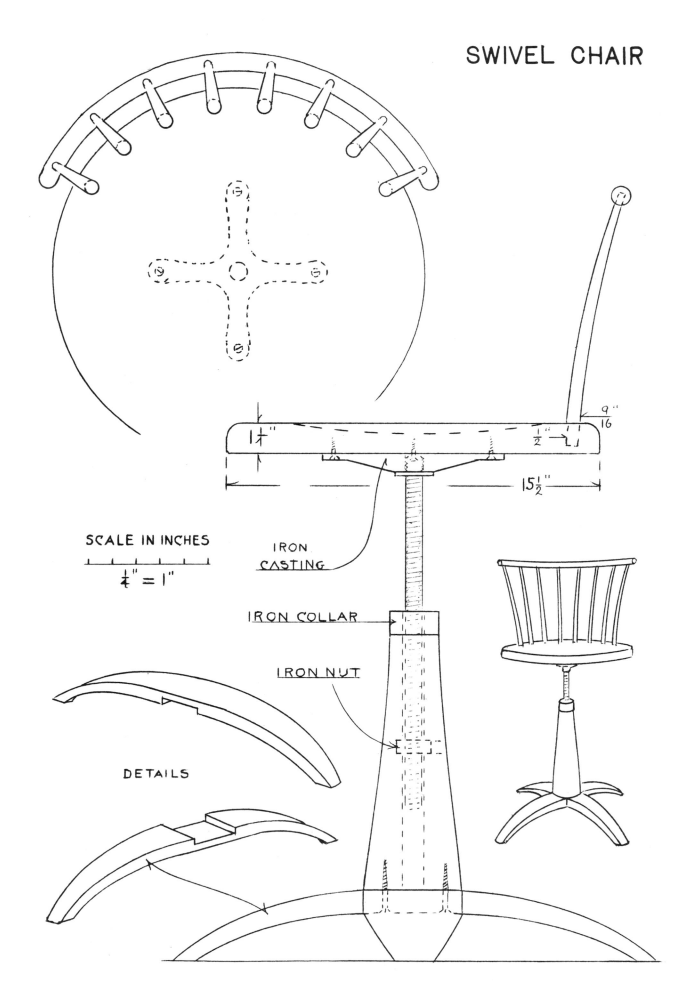

SCALE IN INCHES

$\frac{1}{4}" = 1"$

IRON CASTING

IRON COLLAR

IRON NUT

DETAILS

$1\frac{1}{4}"$

$\frac{1}{2}"$

$\frac{9}{16}"$

$15\frac{1}{2}"$

# REVOLVING STOOL

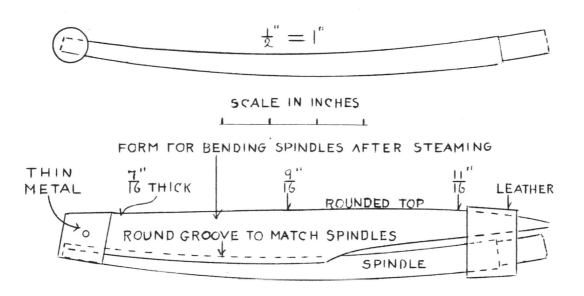

$\frac{1}{2}'' = 1''$

SCALE IN INCHES

FORM FOR BENDING SPINDLES AFTER STEAMING

THIN METAL

$\frac{7}{16}''$ THICK

$\frac{9}{16}''$

ROUNDED TOP

$\frac{11}{16}''$

LEATHER

ROUND GROOVE TO MATCH SPINDLES

SPINDLE

HIGH REVOLVING STOOL

The Shakers made swivel chairs and revolving stools, with their Windsor like turnings, are as modern as our present day functional furniture. The Shakers also called them revolving chairs or just "revolvers". They were made of maple, birch and oak, finished in a dark red stain or left the natural color. By 1863 many were sold to the outside world for use at the piano or sewing machine, with or without a back rest. The price then was 2.50 for a high revolving stool and 2.00 for a pedestal swivel chair.

# MT. LEBANON HIGH CHAIR
## THE SHAKER MUSEUM, OLD CHATHAM, N.Y.

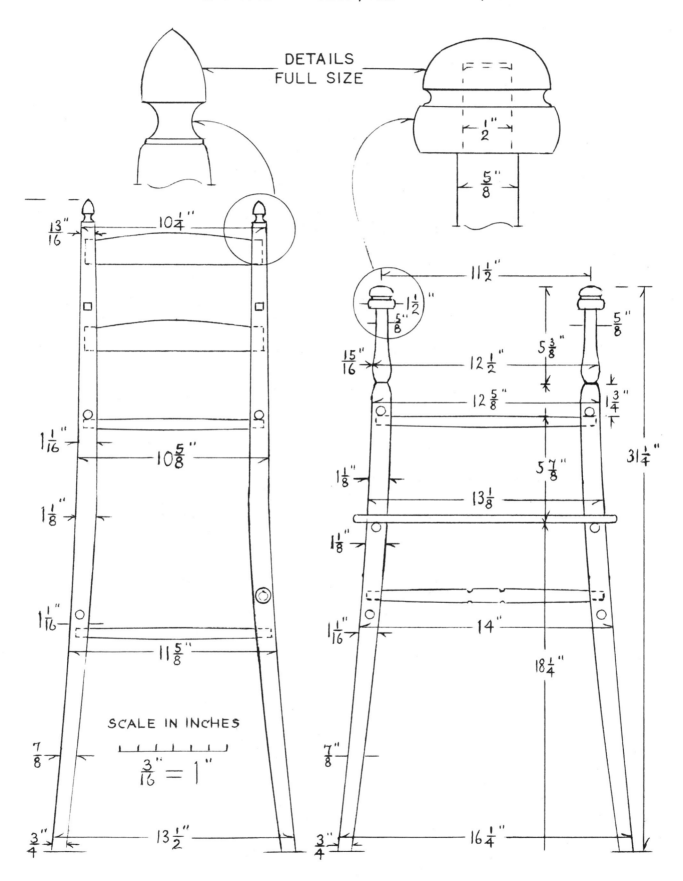

DETAILS
FULL SIZE

SCALE IN INCHES

$\frac{3}{16}" = 1"$

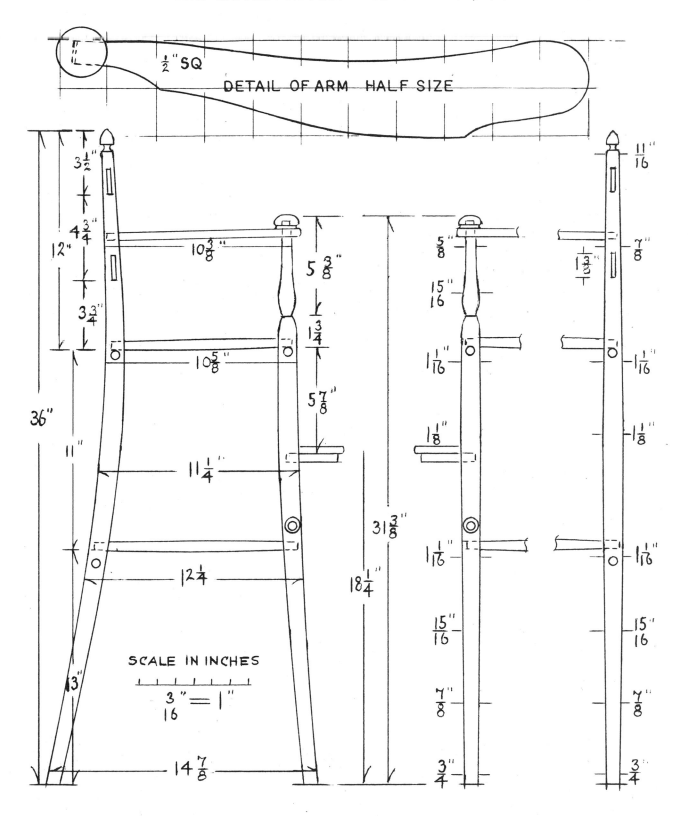

DETAIL OF ARM HALF SIZE

½" SQ

SCALE IN INCHES

$\frac{3}{16}" = 1"$

A few of these Mt. Lebanon high chairs were made in 1880 on spe-
cial order. This unusually graceful chair was made of maple and finished cherry. The design of the chair parts are the same as the
Mt. Lebanon chairs made for sale to the world and shown in their
chair catalog.

These stools were also made like
the sketch, same width but 19½ inches
high. All had taped seats like the
Mt. Lebanon chairs. The stools were
made of maple or birch.

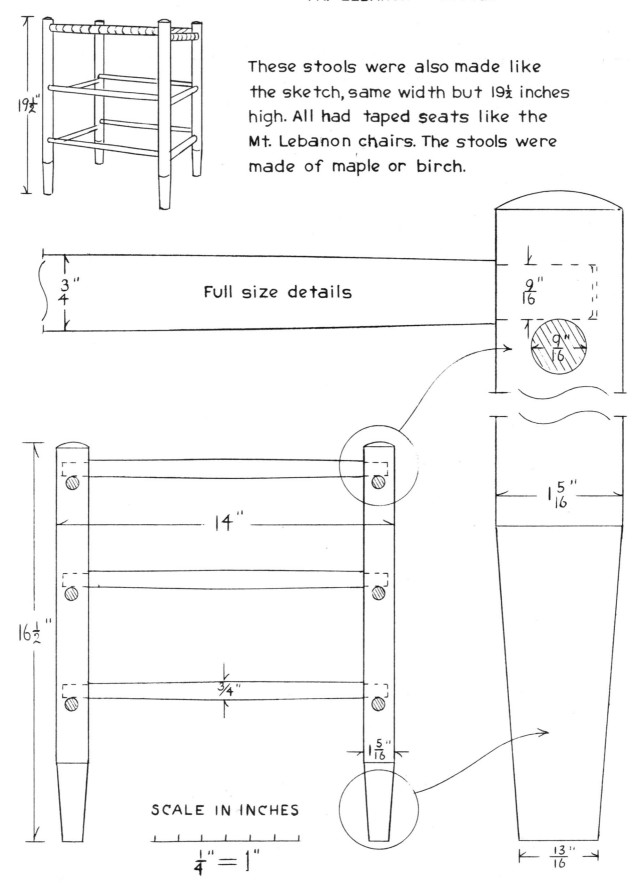

19½"

Full size details

$\frac{3}{4}$"

$\frac{9}{16}$"

$\frac{9}{16}$"

$1\frac{5}{16}$"

14"

16½"

$\frac{3}{4}$"

$1\frac{5}{16}$"

$\frac{13}{16}$"

SCALE IN INCHES

$\frac{1}{4}$" = 1"

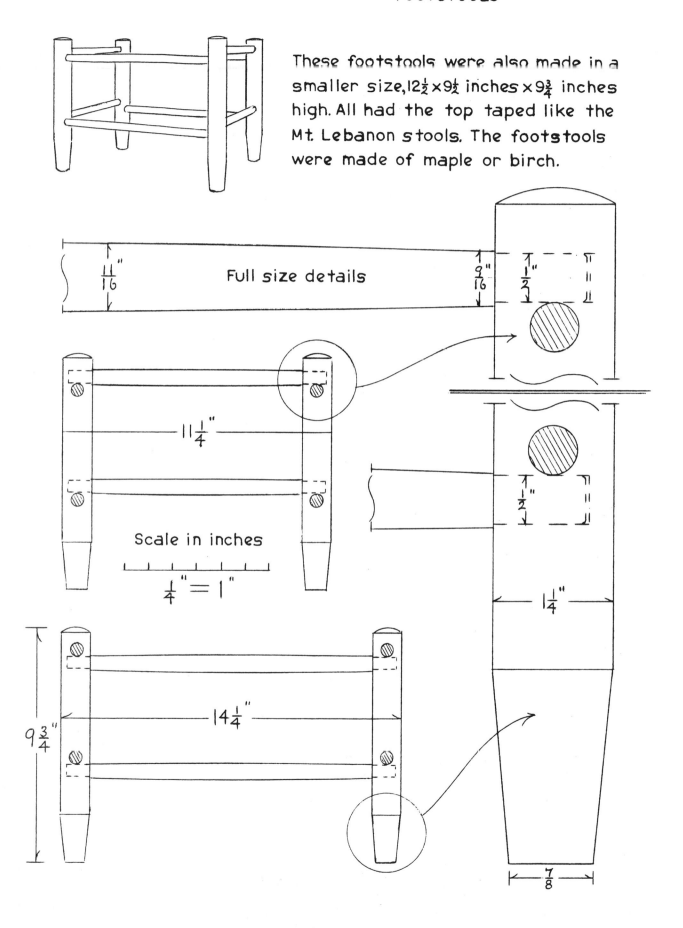

These footstools were also made in a smaller size, 12½ × 9½ inches × 9¾ inches high. All had the top taped like the Mt. Lebanon stools. The footstools were made of maple or birch.

Full size details

$\frac{11}{16}$"

$\frac{9}{16}$"

$1\frac{1}{2}$"

$11\frac{1}{4}$"

$1\frac{1}{2}$"

Scale in inches

$\frac{1}{4}$" = 1"

$1\frac{1}{4}$"

$9\frac{3}{4}$"

$14\frac{1}{4}$"

$\frac{7}{8}$

# CANTERBURY SETTEE

## THE SHAKER MUSEUM, OLD CHATHAM, N.Y.

The plain turned legs, stretchers and back spindles are made of maple, the seat is of pine. The legs are slightly splayed. Because of the lack of a long front stretcher for better strength, I would like to suggest that the the tennons of the two front legs be brought to the top of the seat and properly wedged.

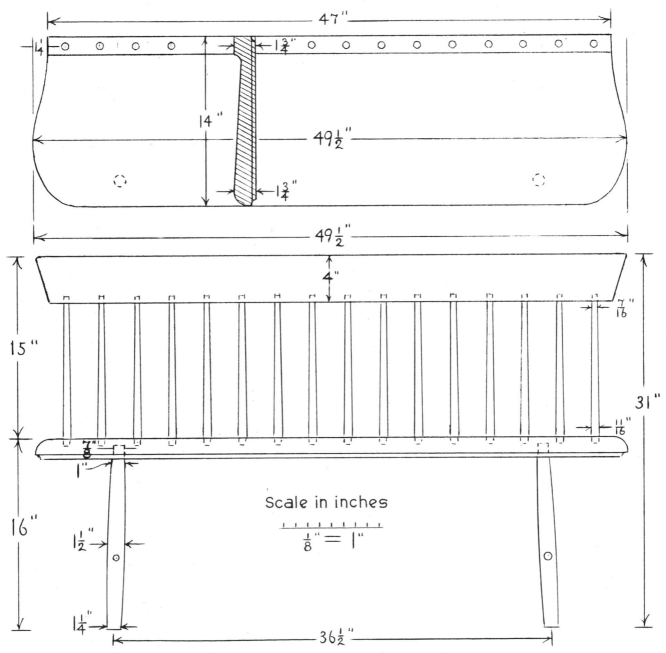

Scale in inches

$\frac{1}{8}" = 1"$

# CANTERBURY SETTEE
## THE SHAKER MUSEUM, OLD CHATHAM, N.Y.

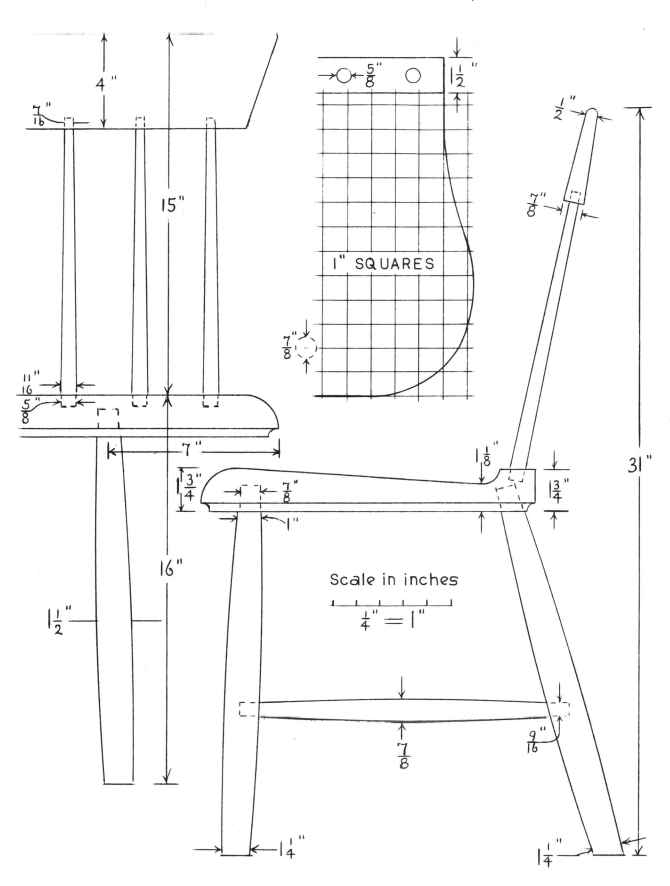

1" SQUARES

Scale in inches

$\frac{1}{4}$" = 1"

# WALL CLOCK
## BY I. N. YOUNGS
### HANCOCK SHAKER VILLAGE, HANCOCK MASS.

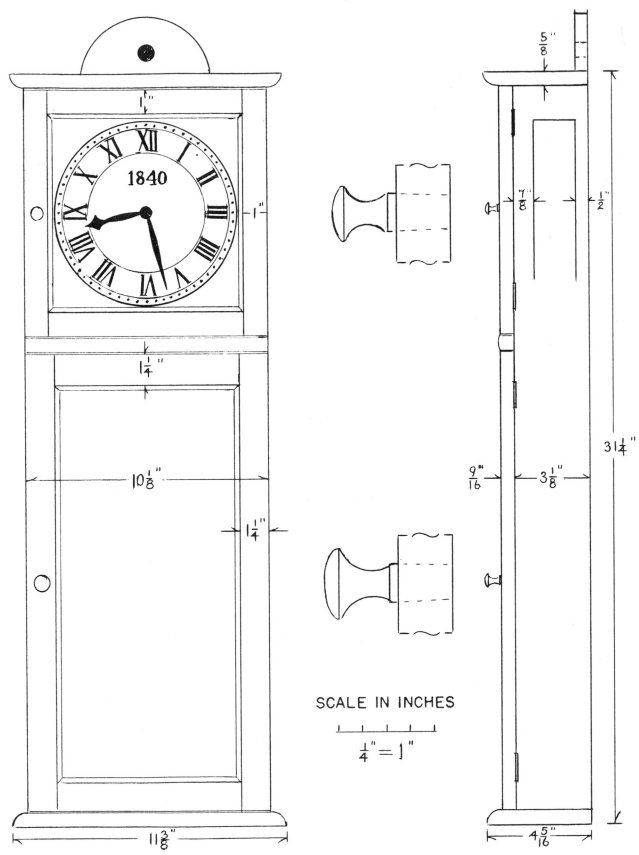

1840

1"

1"

1¼"

10⅛"

1¼"

11⅜"

5/8"

7/8"

1/2"

31¼"

9/16"

3⅛"

4 5/16"

SCALE IN INCHES

¼" = 1"

# WALL CLOCK
## BY I. N. YOUNGS
### HANCOCK SHAKER VILLAGE, HANCOCK MASS.

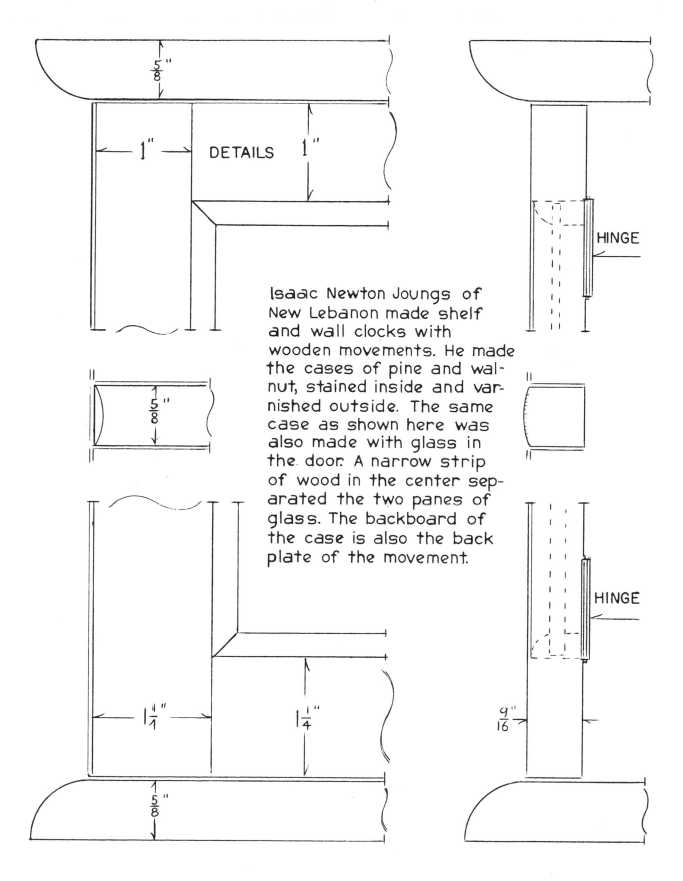

Isaac Newton Joungs of New Lebanon made shelf and wall clocks with wooden movements. He made the cases of pine and walnut, stained inside and varnished outside. The same case as shown here was also made with glass in the door. A narrow strip of wood in the center separated the two panes of glass. The backboard of the case is also the back plate of the movement.

# LOOKING GLASS
From Andrews collection

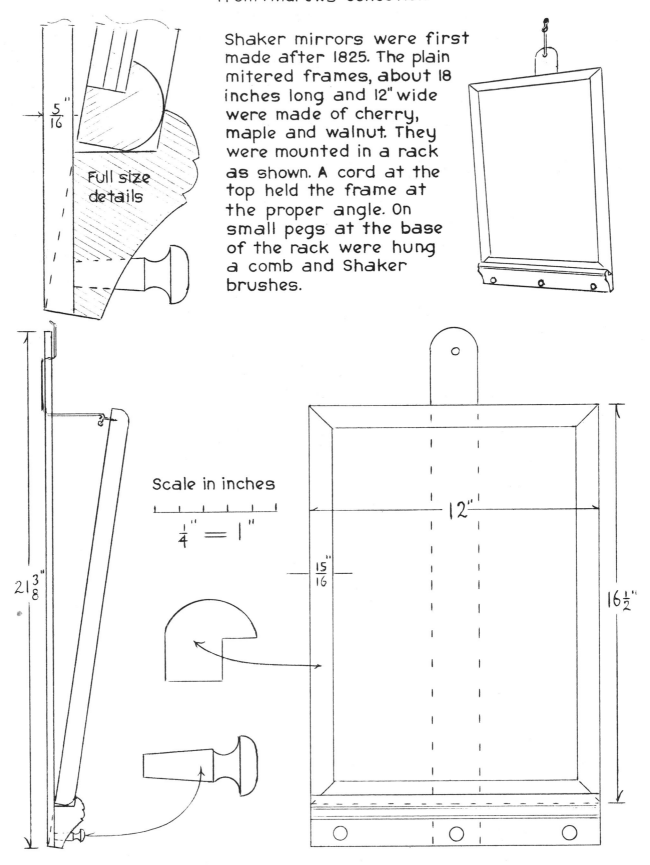

5/16"

Full size details

Shaker mirrors were first made after 1825. The plain mitered frames, about 18 inches long and 12" wide were made of cherry, maple and walnut. They were mounted in a rack as shown. A cord at the top held the frame at the proper angle. On small pegs at the base of the rack were hung a comb and Shaker brushes.

Scale in inches

$\frac{1}{4}$" = 1"

21$\frac{3}{8}$"

12"

15/16"

16$\frac{1}{2}$"

The Shakers made porta-
ble writing desks or writing boxes. Probably made
both for sale and their
own use, they had a place
for paper and and also a
small drawer for an ink-
stand. They were made of
cherry, butternut and pine.
The writing boxes were
made with a flat top.

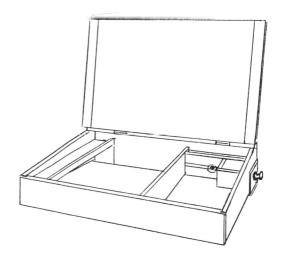

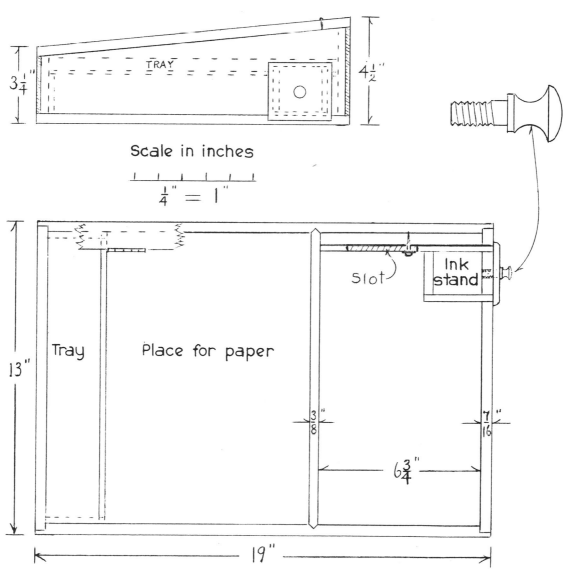

TRAY

$3\frac{1}{4}$"

$4\frac{1}{2}$"

Scale in inches

$\frac{1}{4}$" = 1"

Slot

Ink
stand

Tray

Place for paper

13"

$\frac{3}{8}$"

$\frac{7}{16}$"

$6\frac{3}{4}$"

19"

# SHAKER-MADE WOODENWARE

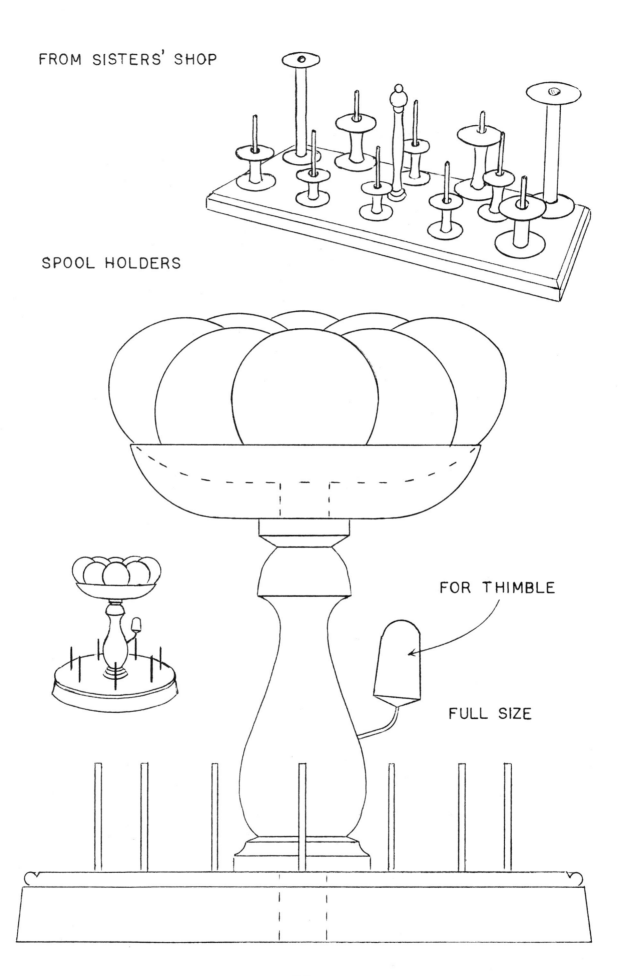

FROM SISTERS' SHOP

SPOOL HOLDERS

FOR THIMBLE

FULL SIZE

60

FROM THE SISTERS' SHOP

1 – Sewing box
2 – Compasses or dividers
3 – Clamp-on pincushion

FROM ANDREWS COLLECTION

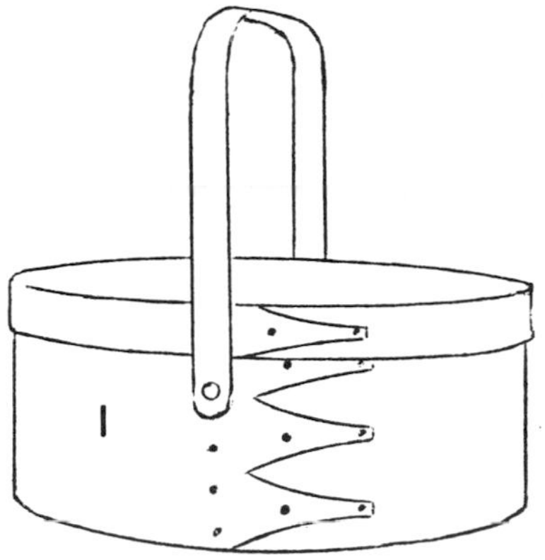

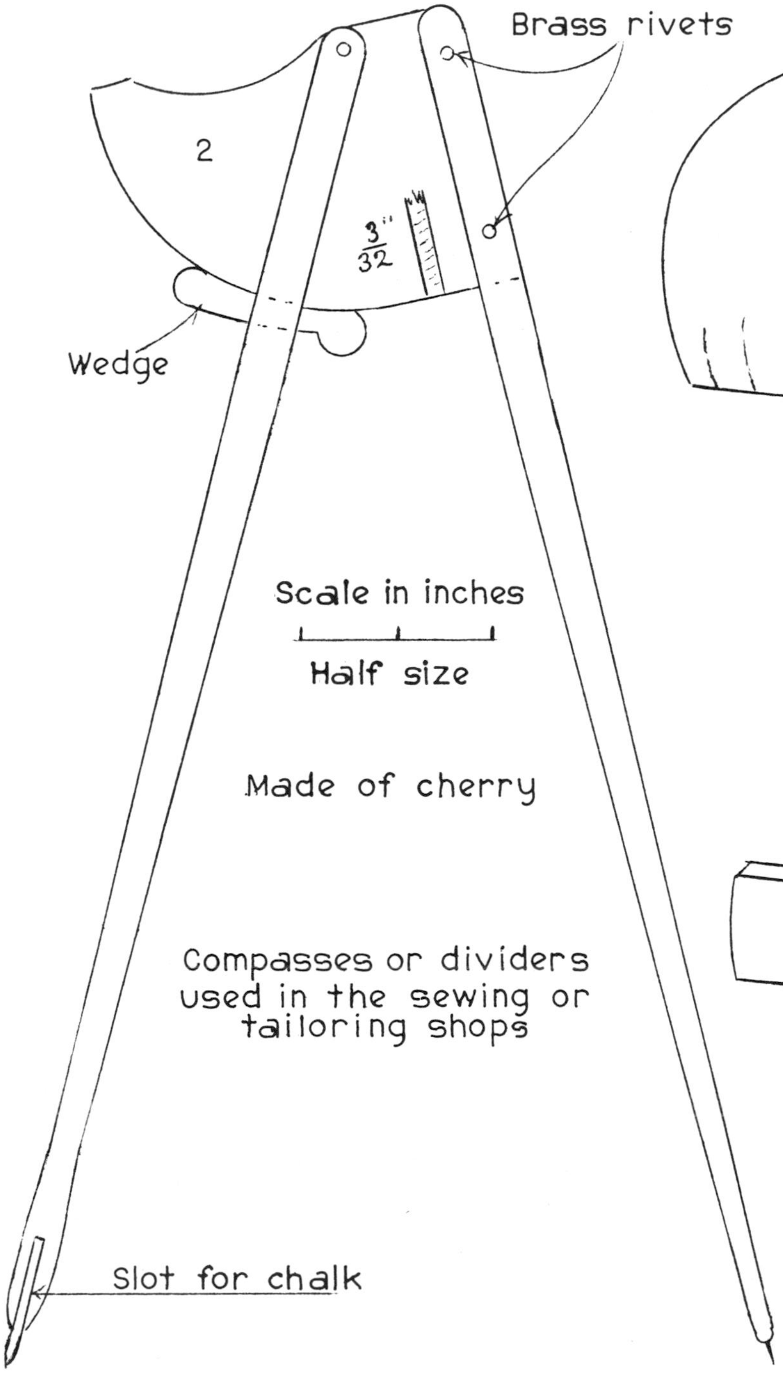

Brass rivets

2

$\frac{3}{32}''$

Wedge

Scale in inches

Half size

Made of cherry

Compasses or dividers
used in the sewing or
tailoring shops

Slot for chalk

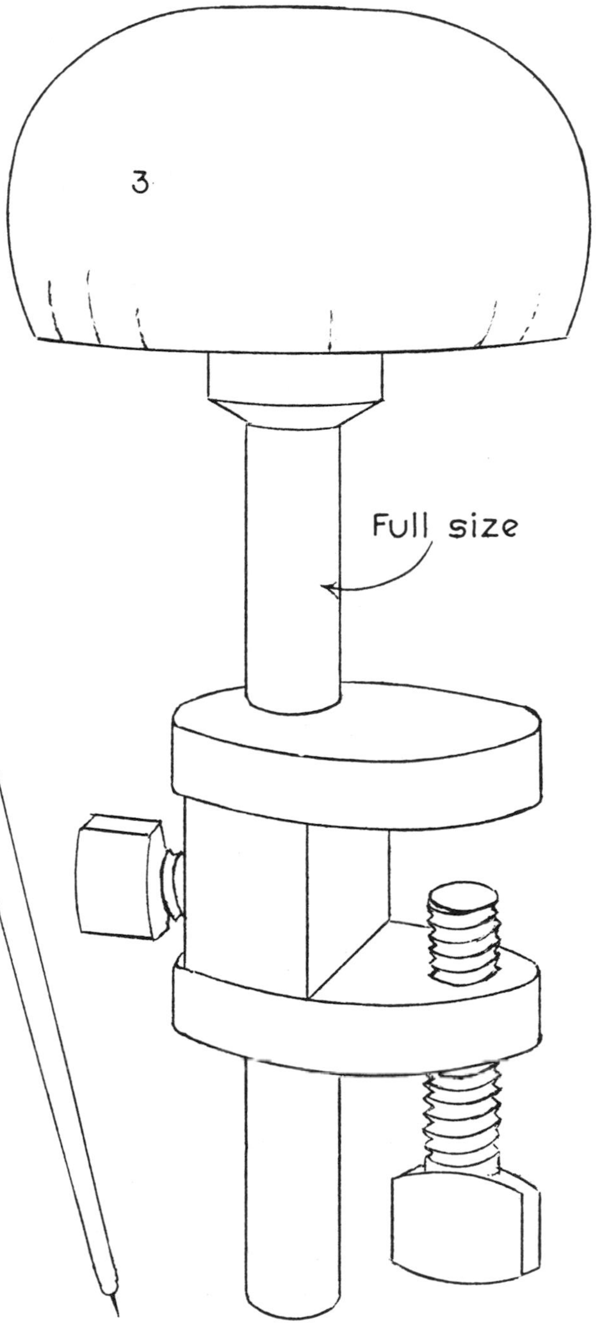

3

Full size

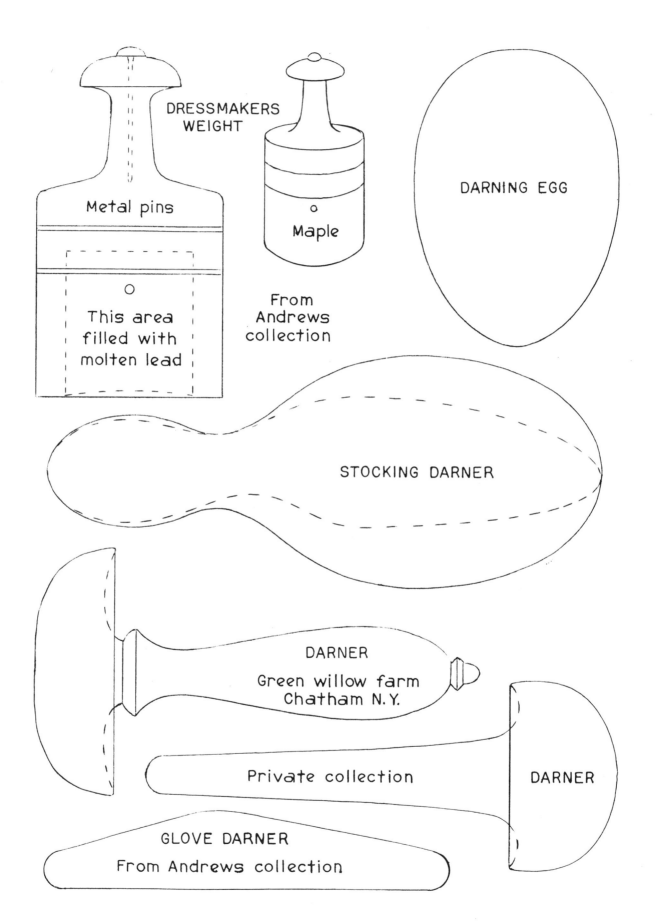

DRESSMAKERS
WEIGHT

Metal pins

This area
filled with
molten lead

Maple

From
Andrews
collection

DARNING EGG

STOCKING DARNER

DARNER

Green willow farm
Chatham N.Y.

Private collection

DARNER

GLOVE DARNER

From Andrews collection

# DIPPERS

The Shakers made dippers to sell from early 1800.
They were made of ash, maple and basswood.

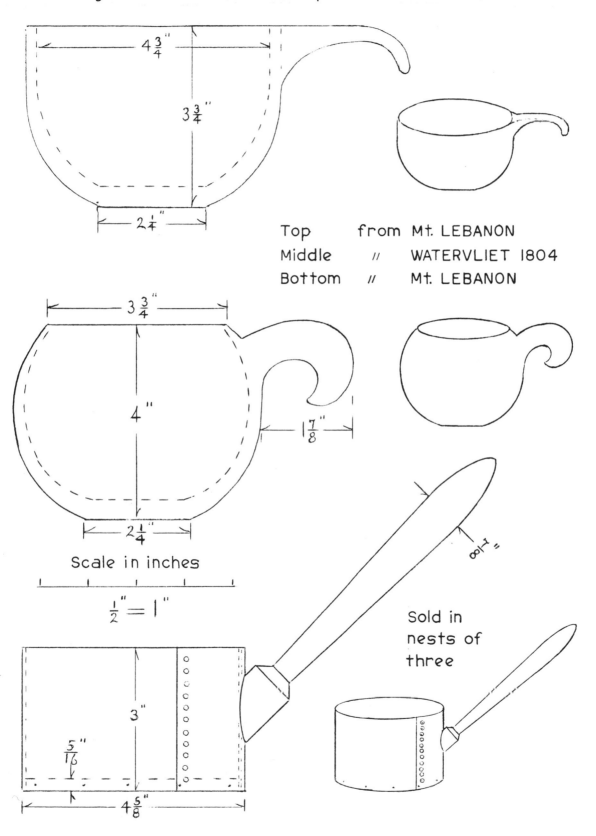

$4\frac{3}{4}"$

$3\frac{3}{4}"$

$2\frac{1}{4}"$

Top      from  Mt. LEBANON
Middle    "     WATERVLIET 1804
Bottom    "     Mt. LEBANON

$3\frac{3}{4}"$

$4"$

$1\frac{7}{8}"$

$2\frac{1}{4}"$

Scale in inches

$\frac{1}{2}" = 1"$

$3"$

$\frac{5}{16}"$

$4\frac{5}{8}"$

$\frac{7}{8}"$

Sold in
nests of
three

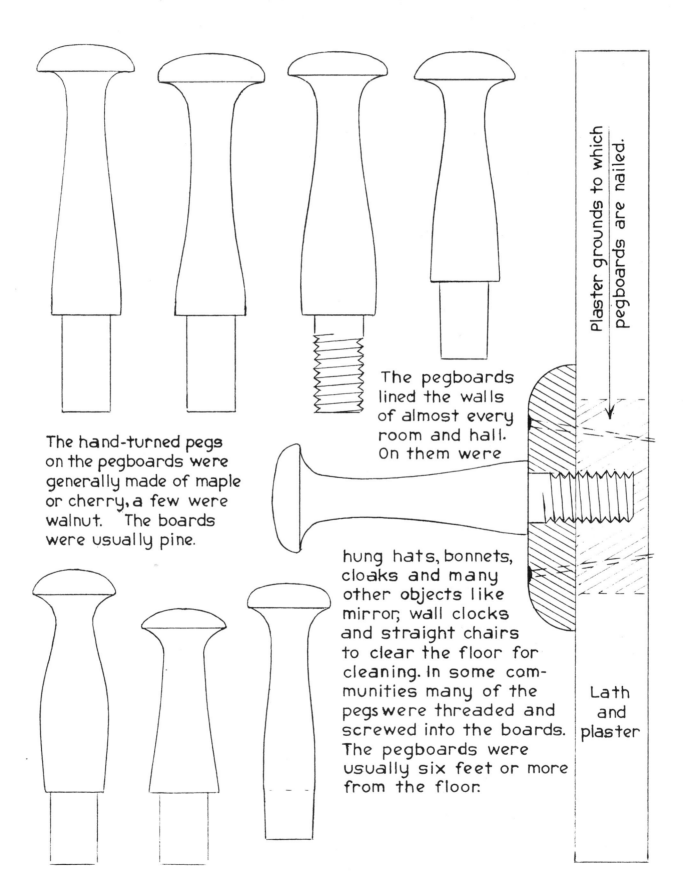

Plaster grounds to which pegboards are nailed.

The hand-turned pegs on the pegboards were generally made of maple or cherry, a few were walnut. The boards were usually pine.

The pegboards lined the walls of almost every room and hall. On them were hung hats, bonnets, cloaks and many other objects like mirror, wall clocks and straight chairs to clear the floor for cleaning. In some communities many of the pegs were threaded and screwed into the boards. The pegboards were usually six feet or more from the floor.

Lath and plaster

# CHAIR FINIALS

Mt. Lebanon
N. Y.

↓ Top of
top slat

Early
Mt. Lebanon
Made to sell

Mt. Lebanon
N. Y.
Made to sell

Early
Mt. Lebanon

Watervliet
N. Y.

↓ Top of
top slat

Hancock
Mass.

Enfield
Conn.

Canterbury
N. H.

# KNOBS AND PULLS

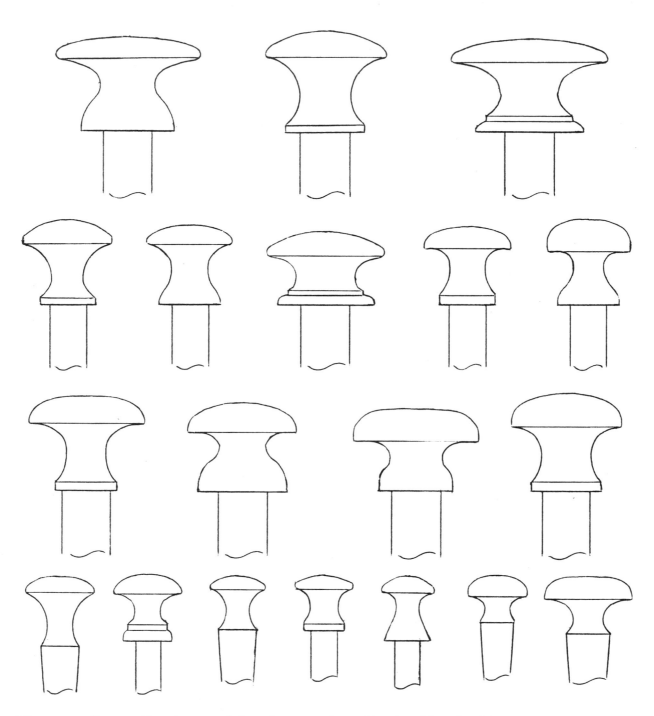

The small neatly turned knobs and pulls in the bottom row were used on clock doors and the drawers in small writing boxes and lap-desks. They were also used as small pegs on the sides of washstands and in the Sisters sewing rooms and kitchen, from which to hang all sorts of small articles and patterns.

# MAPLE BIRCH CHERRY

The beautiful handturned Shaker door knobs and drawer pulls
were turned in a great variety of sizes and shapes to fit all
doors and drawers. They were made of maple, cherry and
walnut

# NEST OF OVAL BOXES

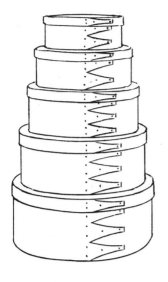

Among many other things made by the Shakers, nothing has been more popular because of its novelty, usefulness and beauty than a nest of oval boxes. At first, the nest consisted of 12 graduated oval boxes, later of 9 and then 7. The oval boxes and carriers, both with or without a cover, and also oval sewing boxes, were made and sold to the outside world continuously for more than 150 years.

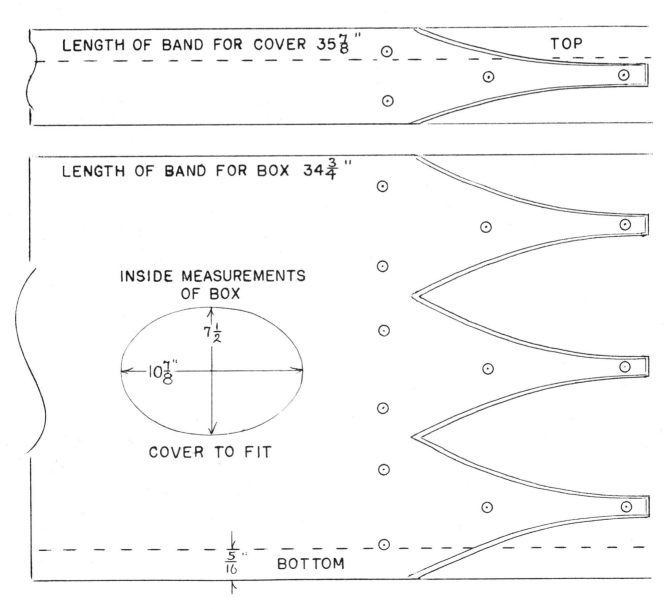

LENGTH OF BAND FOR COVER 35$\frac{7}{8}$"     TOP

LENGTH OF BAND FOR BOX 34$\frac{3}{4}$"

INSIDE MEASUREMENTS OF BOX

7$\frac{1}{2}$

10$\frac{7}{8}$"

COVER TO FIT

$\frac{5}{16}$"   BOTTOM

# NEST OF OVAL BOXES

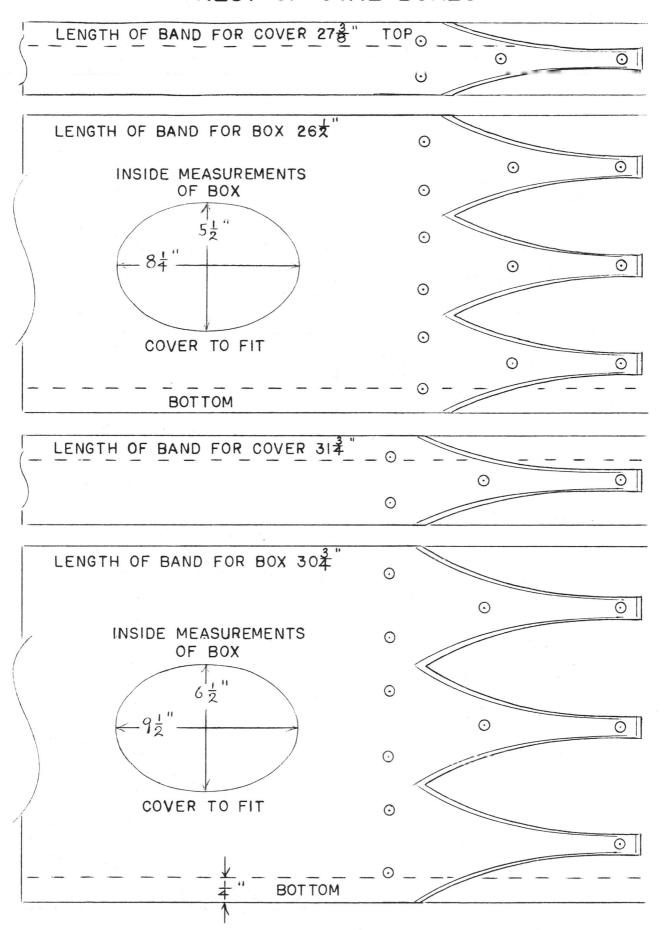

LENGTH OF BAND FOR COVER 27⅜" TOP

LENGTH OF BAND FOR BOX 26½"

INSIDE MEASUREMENTS
OF BOX

5½"

8¼"

COVER TO FIT

BOTTOM

LENGTH OF BAND FOR COVER 31¾"

LENGTH OF BAND FOR BOX 30¾"

INSIDE MEASUREMENTS
OF BOX

6½"

9½"

COVER TO FIT

¼"

BOTTOM

# NEST OF OVAL BOXES

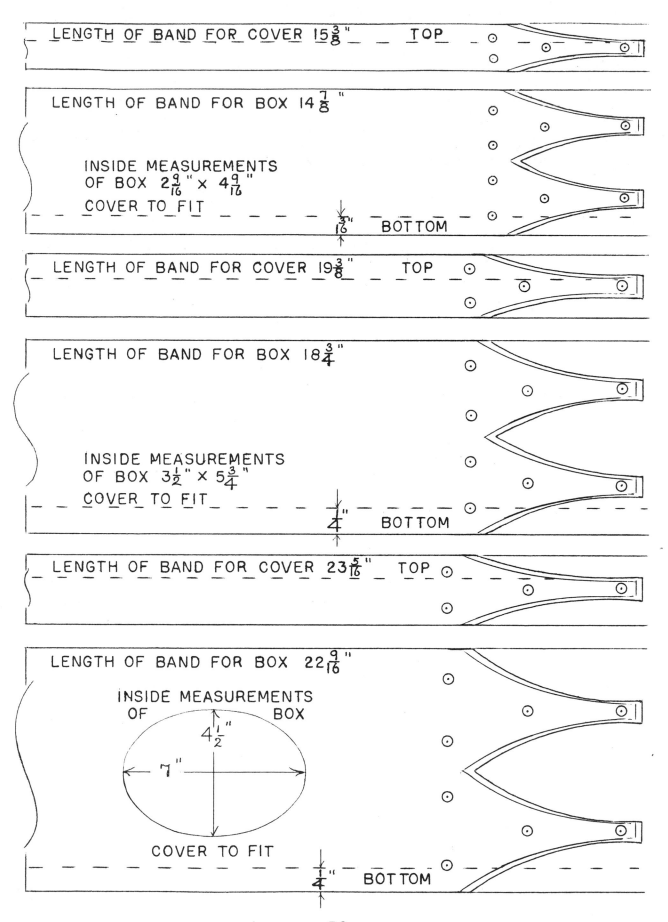

LENGTH OF BAND FOR COVER 15$\frac{3}{8}$" ─ TOP

LENGTH OF BAND FOR BOX 14$\frac{7}{8}$"

INSIDE MEASUREMENTS
OF BOX 2$\frac{9}{16}$" × 4$\frac{9}{16}$"
COVER TO FIT

$\frac{3}{16}$" BOTTOM

LENGTH OF BAND FOR COVER 19$\frac{3}{8}$" ─ TOP

LENGTH OF BAND FOR BOX 18$\frac{3}{4}$"

INSIDE MEASUREMENTS
OF BOX 3$\frac{1}{2}$" × 5$\frac{3}{4}$"
COVER TO FIT

$\frac{1}{4}$" BOTTOM

LENGTH OF BAND FOR COVER 23$\frac{5}{16}$" TOP

LENGTH OF BAND FOR BOX 22$\frac{9}{16}$"

INSIDE MEASUREMENTS
OF                    BOX

4$\frac{1}{2}$"

7"

COVER TO FIT

$\frac{1}{4}$" BOTTOM

70

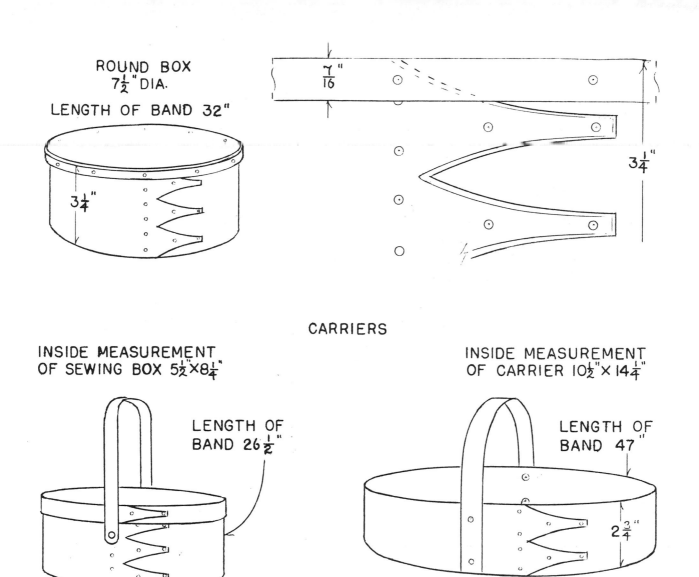

ROUND BOX
7½" DIA.

LENGTH OF BAND 32"

3¼"

$\frac{7}{16}$"

3¼"

CARRIERS

INSIDE MEASUREMENT
OF SEWING BOX 5½"×8¼"

LENGTH OF
BAND 26½"

INSIDE MEASUREMENT
OF CARRIER 10½"×14¼"

LENGTH OF
BAND 47"

2¾"

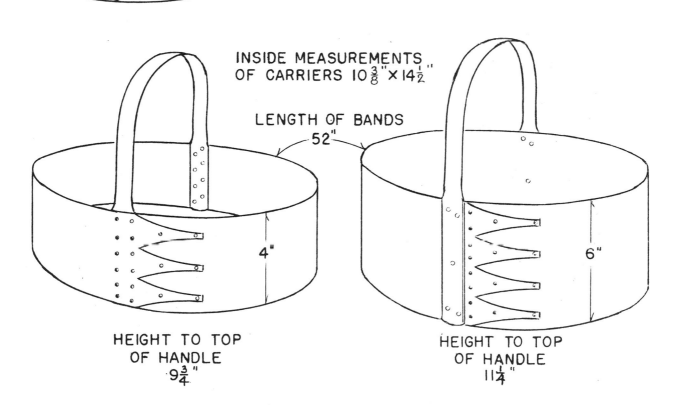

INSIDE MEASUREMENTS
OF CARRIERS 10⅜"×14½"

LENGTH OF BANDS
52"

4"

6"

HEIGHT TO TOP
OF HANDLE
9¾"

HEIGHT TO TOP
OF HANDLE
11¼"

71

# NEST OF OVAL BOXES

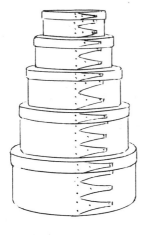

"THAT WHICH HAS IN ITSELF THE HIGHEST USE POSSESSES THE GREATEST BEAUTY"

To make an oval box, or perhaps a nest of oval boxes as the Shakers made them, one must have a solid oval box form or mold, made of wood, one for each size of box to be made. The half-size patterns for 5 different size forms are given below. the same patterns are used for the oval pine bottoms but mark and cut them slightly larger so as to fit them carefully in the boxes.

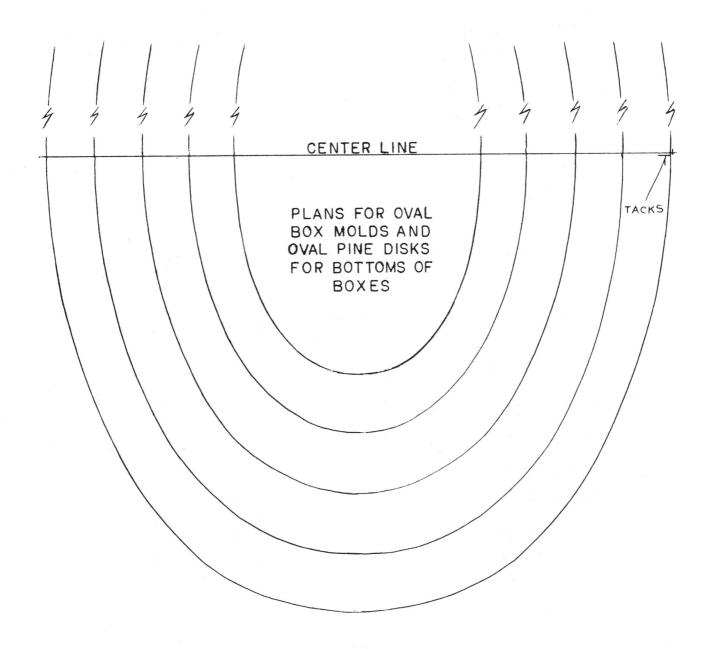

CENTER LINE

PLANS FOR OVAL
BOX MOLDS AND
OVAL PINE DISKS
FOR BOTTOMS OF
BOXES

TACKS

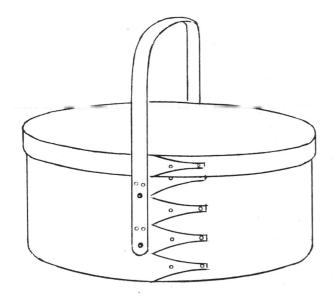

# OVAL BOXES, CARRIERS AND OVAL SEWING BOXES

Most of the molds used by the Shakers were made with 1/8-inch-thick strips of iron inlaid in the proper places, against which to clinch the copper tacks on the inside of the bands. Then they are left on the molds to dry thoroughly. Unless one is going to make oval boxes on a large scale, I would as soon make the molds without the metal strips against which to clinch the copper tacks and just follow the method described below. I have made many dozens of oval boxes and carriers in this manner:

(1) From the patterns, cut to length and width the maple bands for the boxes.

(2) Next, plane and sand to thickness the different bands which are 3/64 to 3/32 inches thick depending upon the size of box.

(3) Then at one end, the fingers or "lappers" are cut with great care according to the patterns.

(4) The opposite end of the bands are planed or sanded for a length of 1 to 2 inches to a 1/64-inch feather edge which helps to make a nice tight fit on the bottom and cover.

(5) Now predrill all the holes for the tacks as laid out on the patterns.

(6) With the oval box molds ready, the maple bands are steamed or soaked in hot water for about an hour and then wrapped tight around the mold. Be sure that the fingers go in the direction shown and also that the vertical centerline row of tacks lines up with the centerline of the box. Find a starting point with a trial wrap. The centerline of the box should be marked on the mold.

(7) When all is right, fasten band tight to oval mold with heavy string or clamps and leave to dry thoroughly.

(8) When dry, and if the band is tight to the mold all around, make a mark on the band at the ends of the fingers before taking it off the mold so that you can then always pull it up to the same dimension.

(9) Now line up and hold it to your marks while drilling through the predrilled holes for a couple of tacks in the centerline row and clinch or peen the tacks on the inside of the box. All the tacks should be very small, no larger than a No. 2 copper tack for the larger boxes. Do the same to the rest of the tacks, leaving the ends of the fingers until last. They are a little delicate to fasten.

(10) After the inside of the box is sanded, the edge-grain pine oval disc is cut a little larger than the oval pattern and carefully fitted into the bottom and fastened with small copper brads without heads. Use the outside of the finished box bottom as a template to make a 1 1/2-inch-thick mold on which to make the cover in the same manner as the box was made, using a selected piece of edge-grain pine for the cover.

The oval boxes and carriers were usually finished with natural varnish. When colors were used instead of varnish, such as a pale yellow or blue, the paint was thinned like a stain, often so light that the grain of the wood was visible. The oval boxes were sold by numbers, the largest size being No. 1.

73

Apothecary cupboard (pages 2,3)

Chest of drawers (pages 6,7)

Work counter (pages 8,9)

74

Candlestand (page 16)

Ejner Handberg

Sewing stand (page 14)

Ejner Handberg

Splayed-leg table (page 21)

Courtesy of Charles L. FLint

Washstand (pages 26, 27)

Ejner Handberg

Washstand (pages 24, 25)

Ejner Handberg

Wood-box (pages 30, 31)

Wood-box (pages 28, 29)

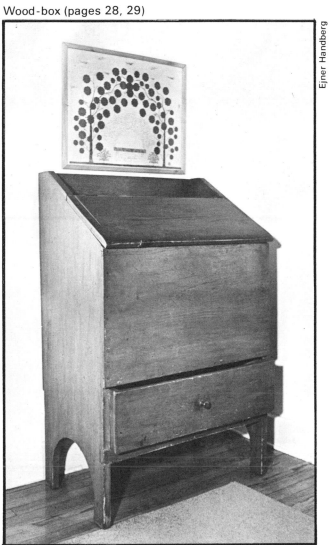

Mt. Lebanon rocking chair No. 0 (pages 38, 39)

Mount Lebanon high chair (pages 48, 49)

Spool holder (page 60)

Spool holder (page 60)

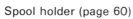

Dipper (page 63)

Nest of oval boxes (pages 68 to 73)

Dividers (page 61)

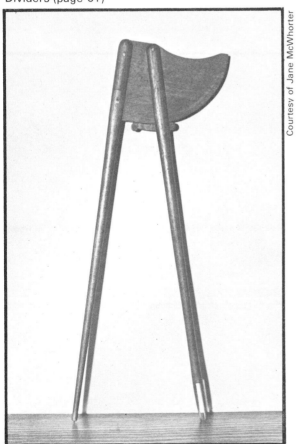

# INDEX

In addition to books on the Shakers and their furniture designs, the Berkshire Traveller Press also publishes books on country inns in North America, Europe, and Britain; on other types of travel; on history, country living, crafts; and cookbooks.

Authors' inquiries are invited; please send a two-to-four-page outline of the work along with a self-addressed, stamped envelope. Unsolicited manuscripts are not accepted.